Complete Pleats

LAURENCE KING

Published in Great Britain in 2015 by

Laurence King Student & Professional
An imprint of Quercus Editions Ltd
Carmelite House
50 Victoria Embankment
London EC4Y 0DZ

An Hachette UK company

Reprinted in 2021

A CIP catalogue record for this book is
available from the British Library

ISBN: 978-1-78067-601-2

10 9 8 7 6 5

Designed by & SMITH
Picture research by Nick Wheldon
Senior Editor: Peter Jones

All original photography by Meidad Sochovolski

Cover design by Pentagram

Printed in China

Papers used by Quercus are from well-managed
forests and other responsible sources.

COMPLETE PLEATS

Pleating Techniques for
Fashion, Architecture
and Design

Paul Jackson

Laurence King Publishing

Contents

1

DIVIDING PAPER

2

BASIC PLEATS

3

TWISTED PLEATS

4

V-PLEATS

5

WORKING WITH GRIDS

6

PLEATS LAID ACROSS PLEATS

7

HOW TO PLEAT FABRIC

Introduction

For millennia, pleats have been used to clothe our bodies and adorn our homes. Although ubiquitous, they have remained largely unregarded, a quiet servant of the decorative and the functional.

However, in recent decades, driven on by new manufacturing techniques, new materials and by the appropriation of origami techniques into design, the humble pleat has undergone a sensational period of rapid development and reassessment. The familiar 'zigzag' has been transformed into a constellation of folded surfaces and forms, made in a wide selection of flexible and rigid sheet materials, across all areas of design. Pleats have become one of the most innovative and exciting of all contemporary design languages. The servant has become the master.

This book attempts to document traditional pleat patterns and their contemporary derivatives systematically. Some of the patterns will be familiar, whereas others will be new. In this way, the book is both a catalogue of known designs and an inspirational collection of new or neglected patterns. It is a one-stop resource for designers who want to use pleats in their work, from fashion to architecture, from jewellery to furniture, and from ceramics to interior design, in sheet materials as diverse as fabric, plastic, metal and laminated wood. The basic patterns are explained in careful detail and then taken through a series of open-ended variations to create a near-endless collection of surfaces and forms, both decorative and functional.

This book draws heavily upon my 30 years' experience teaching pleating to students and to professionals across many design disciplines. Accordingly, I have included only those pleat patterns which I know from experience to be the most versatile, most useful, most teachable and the most beautiful, whether traditional or contemporary. It is simply impossible to include every variation of every pleat pattern – that number must be almost without limit – so instead, the book provides strategies for modifying crease patterns to enable new designs to be created. The diligent reader will notice the occasional overlap of material from my earlier title, *Folding Techniques for Designers: From Sheet to Form*. However, the greater depth and detail of *Complete Pleats* means that pleat patterns from the earlier book have been reclassified in a way that gives them a more accurate technical description and thus greater interconnectivity within the pleat genre. The serious student of folding should consider working from both of these books, which have been written to be mutually complementary.

This book contains numerous examples of inspiring pleated work by contemporary designers from around the world. It also contains work made by students of design who have attended my pleating courses. This is the first time that such a collection has been assembled in print, confirming – should confirmation be needed – that pleats are an indispensable tool for both contemporary designers and for students.

I hope you will enjoy the book and that it will motivate you to create something pleated.

Paul Jackson

This large-scale V-pleat piece of which a detail is shown is made from a variety of processes, including computerized industrial Jacquard weaving and traditional Shibori techniques, using cotton, nylon monofilament and polyester yarns. Dimensions: 60 x 130cm (24 x 52in). Designed by Angharad McLaren (UK).

What is a Pleat?

The word 'pleat' is derived from the Greek *plectos* and the Latin *pli*, *plicare* or *plex*, which means 'fold'. Perhaps surprisingly, there are many words in languages derived from Latin with their origins in a physical or metaphorical meaning of 'fold' or 'unfold', often used in combination with a prefix or suffix such as 'ex-', 'com-', 're-' or '-ment'. These words – in English – include

    ap<u>pli</u>cation
    com<u>plex</u>
    com<u>pli</u>ment
    di<u>plo</u>ma
    du<u>pli</u>cate
    ex<u>plai</u>n
    genu<u>flect</u>
    multi<u>ply</u>
    re<u>flec</u>tion
    re<u>pli</u>ca
    sim<u>pli</u>fy

… and many others. Clearly then, notions of 'to fold' or 'to unfold' are deeply embedded in Latin-based languages and are not confined to paper folding (origami) or pleating. In this sense, the word 'pleat' not only describes a technique for manipulating sheet materials, but it also evokes emotions, abstract thoughts and actions.

However, for our purposes, the word 'pleat' is a catch-all term that describes a furl, corrugation, ruff, drape, crimp, plait, gather, ruck, tuck, dart, ruche or wrinkle, or even plissé, smocking, shirring or gauging, or one of many other specialist artisanal terms originating mostly from the fashion and textile trades and relating specifically to the manipulation of fabric. From country to country and from trade to trade (and sometimes even from studio to studio) there are a great number of local variations on these terms, so for consistency, this book will use the term 'pleat' throughout, in full acknowledgement that some readers may take issue with this simplification.

Description

A pleat is a sheet of material folded back and forth; the pairing – to use terminology borrowed from origami – of a 'valley' fold with a 'mountain' fold. A pleat can be straight or curved, sharp or soft, geometric or organic. It can create a two-dimensional surface or a three-dimensional form; it can be made once, or made as an endless repeat. It can be flexible or rigid, decorative or functional, made from one piece or fabricated from many pieces, and made from one material or from a combination of materials.

So, although the definition of a pleat is simple, the characteristics of the material(s) used and the imagination of the designer can make the realization of a pleat in a designed object unendingly creative.

0.1
The basic pleat, shown open and closed

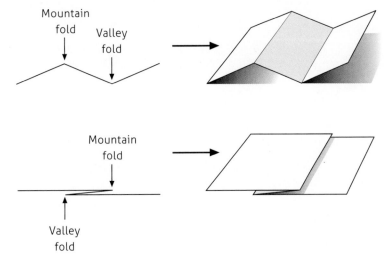

Pleats as Rhythms

Pleat patterns are essentially rhythmic. The basic pairing and equal spacing of a valley fold with a mountain fold will create the familiar accordion pleat (see page 55). This is the simplest pleated rhythm.

The knife pleat (see page 77) is similar to an accordion pleat, but the spacing between the folds is not equal (the knife pleat has been

0.2
The basic accordion pleat

0.3
The knife pleat

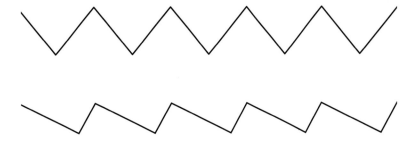

memorably described as 'an accordion pleat with a limp'!). In this way, although the folds are the same as for an accordion pleat, the rhythm is more complex. Thus, the spacing between the folds within a pleat cycle – and also between cycles – can make the rhythm simpler or more complex, as you choose.

The simple two-fold rhythm of the accordion and knife pleat (one valley fold and one mountain fold) can be extended to more complex rhythms of three and four folds, even more, in which valley folds and mountain folds are used in different combinations within each cycle of the repeated rhythm.

These different rhythms can be directly compared to different time signatures in music. A pleat can thus be described as having the rhythm of a polka, waltz, jig or a march, or as having a complex syncopated or jazz tempo. A pleat pattern can be slow and languid, or have a frantic beat, or be anything between. It can be a symphony or a jingle. Thought of in this way – that is, as a musical rhythm – pleat patterns can often be better analysed and categorized than if regarded as an origami crease pattern.

Another system of notation is to sketch possible pleated rhythms on paper. This method creates endless opportunities for experimentation. The examples shown opposite in 0.4 explore pleated surfaces made from combinations of knife pleats and box pleats and are adapted from a page in a student's sketchbook.

Open Pleats and Closed Pleats
_____

When the folds for a pleat pattern have been made, they can often be gathered loosely together so that all the surface of the sheet remains visible, or they can be gathered tightly together and pressed flat, so that only part of the surface of the sheet is visible, the remainder of the material being hidden within the folds of the pleat. These two forms of pleat are known as the 'open pleat' and the 'closed pleat'. Open pleats generally create relief (3D) surfaces, whereas closed pleats generally create flat, layered surfaces.

0.4
Here are some simple examples that show
how the basic pairing of a valley fold with a
mountain fold can be developed. This book
will also provide many other examples.

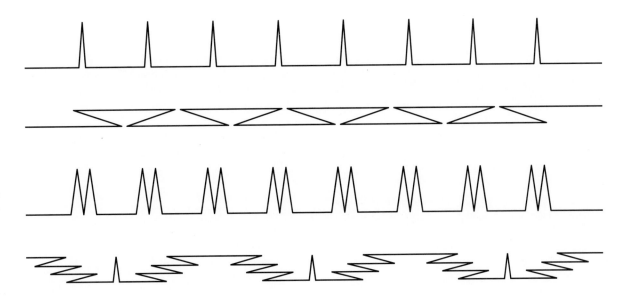

0.5
The 'open' and 'closed' forms of knife pleats
and box pleats.

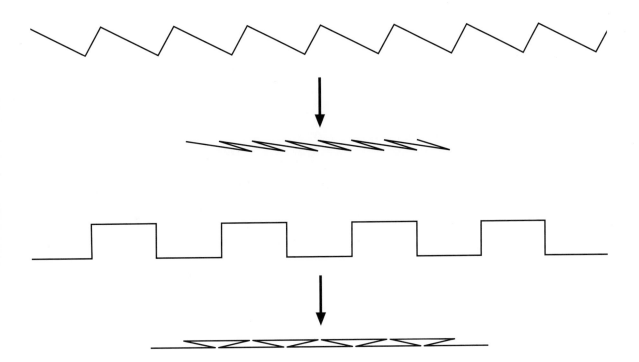

How to Use this Book

Complete Pleats presents generic pleating concepts from which ideas for forms and surfaces can be derived. It is not a book of models to copy, or off-the-peg formulaic solutions for the designer seeking an easy answer to a design problem. This book is useful – or should be – because it presents practical concepts of pleating that can be infinitely adapted by any designer from any design discipline, using any sheet material.

Here are some guidelines to help you move from making samples in the book to creating successful design work.

Materials

The book shows the basic ways in which (usually) a sheet of 90gsm paper can be manipulated into pleated forms, relief surfaces and layered surfaces. It does not show how each of these concepts can be adapted into other sheet materials that are thicker, thinner, softer, harder, larger or smaller, which are stitched, glued or self-supporting, which are one-piece or multipiece, which are handmade or machine-made, which are rigid or flexible, pervious or impervious, tough and hard-wearing or delicate and decorative … and so on and so on, without end. (Although it does show how pleats can be made with fabric – see Chapter 7, 'How to Pleat Fabric', page 280.) These are decisions that you must make as a designer. The adaptation of a pleat into a material that is not paper can radically change how even the simplest pleat looks. In this way, the material is as important as the pleat pattern, sometimes more so. The integration of the right

material with the right pleat pattern (and with a good idea) will always create the best design work.

The gallery sections will show many of these technical and material possibilities, but lack of space prevents any detailed discussion of how each piece was made.

Play a Lot

The best approach to using this book successfully is to play. Don't just make one example, look at it briefly, then turn the page to make another example. Instead, play with what you have made, fold it this way and that; press the pleats flat or stretch them open along one edge, then along a second edge, then press two edges together at the same time; squeeze flat or stretch open the middle; turn it around and around in your two hands to look at it from all angles. From long experience, it is often more fruitful to make one pleat design and play with it in your hands for five minutes, than to make five different designs and expect to find a quick solution from one of them, but without playing diligently with any of the five.

From each example given in the book, an immense number of related examples can be made. However, don't just imagine what they would look like … make as many as you can. If you can't fully understand how to make something because you can only partly understand, try anyway, making things up as you go along, changing your mind as you go. You may not make your original idea exactly, but you may well make something better than you could (or couldn't) conceive of when you began. Pleat patterns can look somehow pre-determined, immutable and unchangeable, but when you begin to create variations, you will see how wonderfully malleable they are, both as a crease pattern and as a physical form. So ... you are very strongly encouraged to play, play, play!

It is Not Important to be a Folding Virtuoso

Do not feel frustrated if you attempt to make the more complex examples in the book, but cannot. They look spectacular, but the truth is – perhaps paradoxically – that they are also the least useful pleat patterns in the book. Instead, make the simpler, less showy examples, because they will offer you more creative possibilities in a greater choice of materials. It is easy to be seduced by complex pleats with a wow factor, but generally, the more complex a folding pattern is to make, the more specific will be the final result, and thus the less versatile. When working with pleats – as in all matters of design – less is often more (more or less).

Remember: you are first and foremost a designer using pleats, not a pleating specialist trying to be a designer. If all you can make is the simplest accordion pleat, but you make it beautifully, in absolutely the right material, and your design has a strong concept, you will create a wonderful piece of work. Always put a pleating pattern at the service of the design concept, not the other way round.

Fold a Lot

Of course, not everything extrapolated from the examples in this book will be immediately successful. Much of what you create initially will probably be technically or aesthetically weak – many pieces will only become successful after a process of much refinement. In this sense, designing with pleats is no different to any other design process. This book is absolutely not a quick-fix substitute for perseverance and hard work.

Be sure to read the first chapter, 'Dividing Paper' (page 20). It is extremely important. If you take a little time to learn how to divide paper accurately, the possibilities for what you can create will become almost unlimited, and relatively easy.

In truth, there is absolutely no substitute for folding, folding, folding. Thinking too much, analysing too much and trying to understand in your head what something will look like will inevitably discourage you, or at the very least lead to poor design work. Paper is readily available, quick and easy to work with, and very inexpensive. Use it – and use this book – as extensively as time permits before perhaps adapting your ideas into other materials.

How to Make the Examples

There are four ways to make the examples you see in this book. Which method you use for which example depends on personal taste and on the characteristics of the example being made.

Like developing ideas in a sketchbook, the key to developing good designs with pleats is to work fluently and quickly; your folding does not always need to be technically perfect (yes, really!). A great deal of time can be saved by working somewhat roughly, then remaking something with care when you feel you have an idea worth developing. Don't allow yourself to become bogged down in unnecessarily precise folding of a pleat pattern with 30 repeats when all you need is a quickly made folded sketch with five repeats. Working too slowly and in too much detail is typical of a beginner. With experience, your speed and spontaneity with paper will increase. Here are the four methods for making:

1. Folding by Hand

Folding by hand is as low-tech as any making activity can be. It is the original 'digital art' (*digitus* is Latin for 'finger'). You are making something directly with your body (your hands) without the intervention of a third-party tool such as a pencil, mouse or needle. It is an almost unique making experience and perhaps unfamiliarly primal. This very basic, hands-on activity – especially in today's high-tech design studio environments – can be a very powerful and rewarding experience for both the rawest student and the most seasoned professional, and should not be underestimated or regarded as unsophisticated or inadequate. You can think of folding by hand as an alternative to designing by computer (which means that aside from the design benefits, folding by hand is of itself an excellent educational experience).

Many of the examples in this book are made from paper divided into 8, 16 or 32. These divisions are quick and easy to make by hand (see the 'Dividing Paper' chapter), and learning how to make them will save you a great deal of time spent measuring with a ruler.

Think of folding by hand as the norm, resorting to using the other methods described below only when necessary.

By carefully selecting specific folds in specific sections of a dense grid of horizontal, vertical and diagonal folds, similar to the grid described on page 231, the modified grid will collapse to create this spectacular twisting column, made in paper. The piece is very flexible, able to bend, twist, stretch and compress in many directions. Dimensions: 73 x 23 x 23cm (30 x 9 x 9in). Designed by Andrea Russo (Italy).

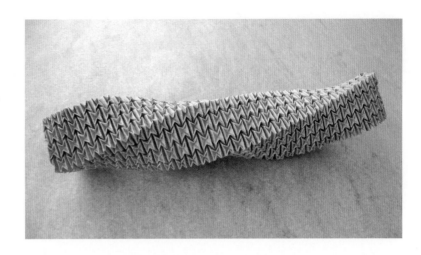

2. Using Geometry Equipment

Simple geometry equipment such as a scalpel or craft knife, a ruler, a pair of compasses, 360-degree protractor and a hard, sharp pencil are sometimes necessary to help construct unusual shapes of paper, precise angles, incremental divisions, etc. However, be careful that using them doesn't become habitual, so that you find yourself using them when folding something by hand would be quicker and easier.

3. Using a Computer

These days, most of us would prefer to draw folding patterns on a computer, rather than to draw them on paper with geometry equipment. We seem to be losing the 'hands on' habit. However, drawing on a computer does have its advantages: scaling is easy, as is symmetrical repetition, or skewing or stretching, and drawings can be kept and copied endlessly.

The biggest drawback is having to print out your drawing. If it is bigger than the size of your printer, you may have to collage sections of the drawing together, which can be messy and imprecise. The alternative is to use a plotter. If you don't have ready access to one, many walk-in print and copy shops have a plotter and can make inexpensive black-and-white copies a metre or so wide.

4. Combining Methods

Being pragmatic, switching between the three methods described above is probably the way that most people will make most of the examples, most of the time. Each has its advantages and disadvantages, and experience will tell you when to use which method.

How to Work from the Drawings, Photographs and Text

The Drawings

Unless stated in the text, the exact lengths and angles used in a drawing are unimportant. As long as what you make looks something like the drawing, it will be accurate enough. Where an element of the construction is critical, this will be stated and you should follow the instructions exactly. If a shape is clearly a circle, or edges or angles are clearly at 90 degrees (or whatever) this may not be stated, so do the obvious and make what your eyes can see. Think of the drawings as suggestions rather than as models to copy.

However, rather than eyeball a drawing and draw it freehand without references, it may be helpful to first use a ruler and measure its major lines. This will give you a rough sense of its proportion, and then it can be scaled up to the appropriate size.

One tip when making something for the first time is to avoid making it very small. Samples that are small can look trivial and be creatively inhibiting, and you may feel like your time has been wasted. Similarly, if you make things too big they can look clumsy and weak. As a rough guide, try to make samples that can fit on to an A4 sheet (8 x 11¾in). Later, when you know the scale you want and the sheet material you want to work with, you can make them at the correct scale, larger or smaller.

The Photographs

Although the photographs were taken to make the examples look interesting and attractive (of course), their primary function is to give descriptive information about how the different planes, edges and folds lie in relation to each other, so that you have a better sense of how something should look when made. In that sense, the photographs should be regarded as explanatory diagrams, not simply as pleasing pictures that attempt to beautify the book.

Paper is a living, breathing material. It distorts under the heat of studio lights, reacts to humidity and can bend out of symmetry, depending on the direction of the grain (the direction of the parallel fibres that lie within the paper). For these reasons, some of the folded examples may look a little misshapen. The alternative to seeing an occasional wobble was to make everything from thick card that would not distort. However, this was considered a rather soulless material for the book. The idiosyncrasies of paper are hopefully more appealing, giving the folded forms a little personality.

The Text

Read it! With a book such as this, which is primarily visual, it is tempting to dive straight into making a project without first reading about its structure or merit for being included in the book. However, the more reading you do – and preferably in sequence through the book, from beginning to end – the greater will be your understanding of what you make. From this greater knowledge, greater success will follow.

So, if you find yourself wondering what the coloured lines mean, or what the loopy arrows mean, or why such-and-such a pleat pattern precedes another, calm your itchy fingers and please read more.

How to Cut and Fold

Cutting

If you are cutting paper or card by hand, it is important to use a quality craft knife or, better still, a scalpel. Avoid using the inexpensive 'snap-off' craft knives, as they can be unstable and dangerous; the stronger, chunkier snap-off knives are more stable and much safer. However, for the same price you can buy a scalpel with a slim metal handle and a packet of replaceable blades. Scalpels are generally more manoeuvrable through card than craft knives and will help you to create a more accurate cut line. Whichever knife you use, it is imperative to change the blade regularly.

A metal ruler or straight edge will ensure a strong, straight cut, although transparent plastic rulers are acceptable and have the added advantage that you can see the drawing beneath them. Use a nifty 15cm (6in) ruler to cut short lines. Generally, when cutting, place the ruler on the drawing, so that if your blade slips away it will cut harmlessly into the waste card around the outside of the drawing.

It is also advisable to invest in a self-healing cutting mat. If you cut on a sheet of thick card or wood, the surface will quickly become scored and rutted, and it will become impossible to make straight, neat cuts (see page 18).

Folding

While cutting card is relatively straightforward, folding is less so. Whatever the method you use, the crucial element is never to cut through the material along the fold line but, by using pressure, to compress the fold line. This is done using a tool. Whether the tool is purpose-made or improvised is a matter of personal choice and habit.

Bookbinders use a range of specialist creasing tools called 'bone folders'. They compress card very well, though the fold line is usually 1–2mm ($\frac{1}{25}$–$\frac{1}{12}$in) or so away from the edge of the ruler, so if your tolerances are small, a bone folder may be considered inaccurate.

A good improvised tool is a dry ballpoint pen. The ball makes an excellent crease line, though like the bone folder, it may be a little distance away from the edge of the ruler. I have also seen people use a scissor point, an eating knife, a tool usually used for smoothing down wet clay, a fingernail (!) and a nail file.

My own preference is a dull scalpel blade (or a dull craft knife blade). The trick is to turn the blade upside down. It compresses the card along a reliably consistent line, immediately adjacent to the edge of the ruler.

A scalpel is here shown held in the standard position for cutting. For safety, be sure to always keep your non-cutting hand topside of your cutting hand.

A craft knife makes an excellent tool with which to create a fold. Held upside down against the edge of a ruler, it does not cut the card along the length of the fold line, but compresses it.

Equipment

The designs in this book are all simple to measure and to construct. Accuracy in the making is essential, but accuracy does not come from a state of mind or some inborn talent. Instead, it comes from a willingness to be careful and – most importantly – from using equipment that is clean and of reasonable quality.

Here is a list of the basic equipment you will need:
• Hard pencil (2H is good). Keep it sharp!
• Good eraser (not the one on the end of your pencil)
• Good pencil sharpener if your pencil is not mechanical
• 15cm (6in) plastic ruler
• 30cm (12in) metal or plastic ruler
• Large 360-degree protractor
• Quality craft knife or scalpel, with replacement blades
• Invisible tape and/or masking tape (for healing mistakes)
• Self-healing cutting mat, as large as possible

The above equipment – with one exception – can be purchased very inexpensively; your total outlay will probably be less than a third of the price of this book. As with most things, it pays to buy items of quality, although it is more important to use equipment that is inexpensive but clean, rather than equipment that is expensive but dirty. Age-old grime on a ruler or protractor will quickly transfer to your paper or card and make everything you create look grubby and trivial. Work cleanly and you will work more accurately, with more care and with more motivation.

The one relatively expensive item is a self-healing cutting mat. It is pure vandalism to cut through paper or card on a tabletop, and the alternatives of wood or thick card quickly become rutted and problematic. A specialist cutting mat will ensure that every cut line runs straight and smooth. Buy the biggest you can afford. If it is looked after carefully, it will remain in good condition for a decade or more. A nice bonus with a cutting mat is that it will have a grid of centimetres and/or inches printed on it, meaning that for some constructions you will rarely, if ever, need to measure with a ruler.

Symbols

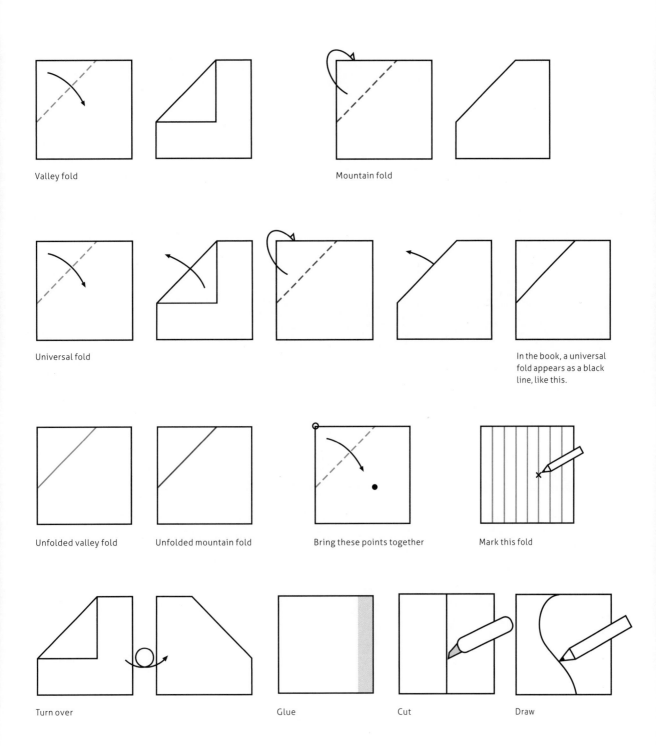

Valley fold

Mountain fold

Universal fold

In the book, a universal fold appears as a black line, like this.

Unfolded valley fold

Unfolded mountain fold

Bring these points together

Mark this fold

Turn over

Glue

Cut

Draw

1

DIVIDING PAPER

Dividing Paper

Learning quick and easy ways to divide paper is the essence of making pleats. If you can fluently divide paper, then the world of pleating will open up. If, on the contrary, you skip learning this simple skill, making pleats will forever be slow, difficult and frustrating.

You are very strongly advised to refrain from diving deep into the book to make something spectacular and instead to spend time in this chapter learning the basics of dividing paper. Once the basics have been learnt, you will be able to make anything in the book, simple or complex, 2D or 3D. You will also be able to create your own patterns.

If your final material of choice is not paper, but fabric, or plastic or even the façade of a building, then clearly, you cannot easily divide those materials, if at all. In that sense, learning to divide paper may seem like a redundant skill. But you would be wrong.

Learning to divide means that you can experiment, change your mind, make mistakes, invent, take risks and make maquettes. Further, the methods described in this chapter enable you to divide accurately, meaning that you will achieve perfect results, every time.

So, curb your enthusiasm and take the time you need to learn how to divide into eight, sixteen, thirty-two, sixty-four as valleys and as mountain-valley pleats. Every minute spent in this seemingly unglamorous chapter will enable you to fold and create for an unlimited number of hours afterwards. Dividing paper is a tool and we cannot make anything without tools.

1.1

Linear Divisions

There are two different ways to partition a sheet of material into equal divisions: linear divisions and rotational divisions. This section will describe linear divisions; rotational divisions are described later in the chapter.

1.1_1
A linear division partitions the *length* of a sheet of material into equal segments that progress in a straight line from one end to the opposite end. The length can be any size, and it can be divided into any number of equal segments.

Linear Division

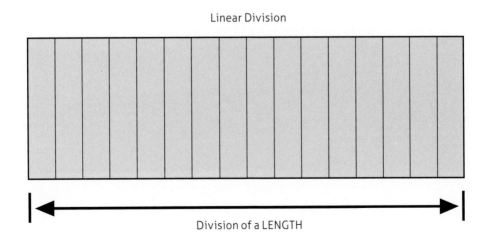

Division of a LENGTH

1.1.1   Dividing into Valleys Only

Before beginning to create pleats that combine valley folds and mountain folds,it is extremely useful to learn the principles of how to divide paper using valley folds only. The exercises that follow are essential to an understanding of how to create linear pleats and should be learnt well.

1.1.1.1   Valley Sixteenths

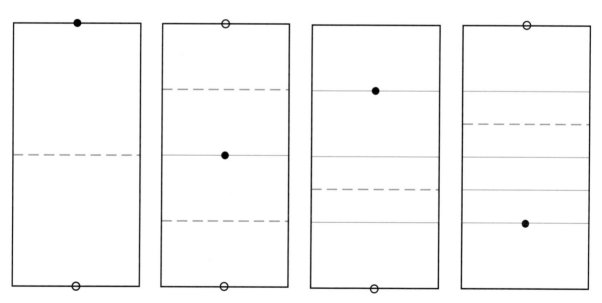

1.1.1.1_1
Fold the ○ edge to the ● edge, folding the paper in half. Open the paper.

1.1.1.1_2
Fold the edges to the centre line. Open the paper.

1.1.1.1_3
Fold the ○ edge to the ● crease. Open the paper.

1.1.1.1_4
Fold the ○ edge to the ● crease. Open the paper.

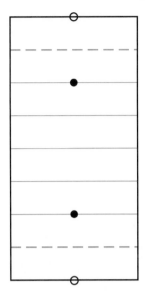

1.1.1.1_5
Fold the ○ edges to the ●
creases. Open the paper.

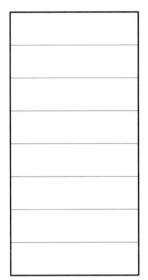

1.1.1.1_6
There are now seven valley
folds that divide the paper into
equal eighths.

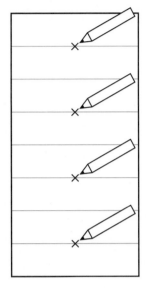

1.1.1.1_7
With a pencil, discreetly mark
each alternate valley crease
with an X.

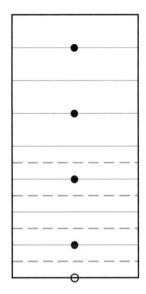

1.1.1.1_8
Fold the ○ edge in turn to all
the X creases (●) marked in Step
7, making four new folds. Open
the paper after each new fold.

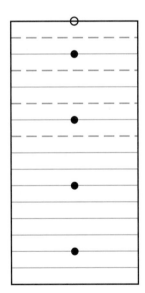

1.1.1.1_9
Repeat Step 8 with the other
edge of the paper. Be careful
to fold the edge only to the
four marked creases.

1.1.1.1_10
This is the completed division of
the paper into linear sixteenths.

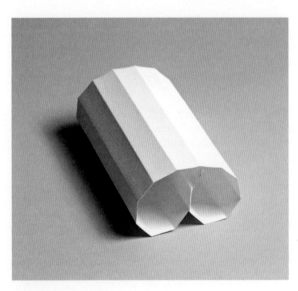

The paper is divided into
sixteenths, using valley folds
only. The result is a curled
cylinder, not a pleat.

1.1.1.2 Valley Thirty-seconds

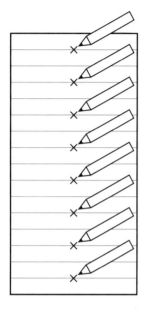

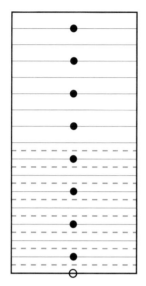

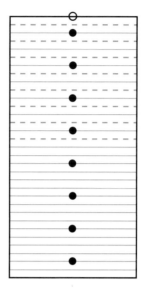

1.1.1.2_1
Begin by making the valley
sixteenths. With a pencil, mark
an X on each alternate crease.
There will be eight Xs. Do not
mark a ● as on the previous
page, as this will muddle the old
marks with the new ones and
create confusion.

1.1.1.2_2
Fold the ○ edge to each X crease,
marked here with a ●. There will
be eight new folds.

1.1.1.2_3
Repeat with the other edge,
creating eight more new folds.

1.1.1.2_4
This is the completed division
of the paper into linear
thirty-seconds.

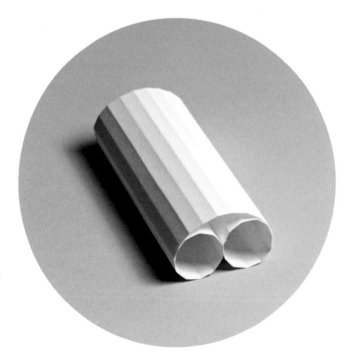

With 32 divisions, the paper
curls tighter than with the
16 divisions seen in the
previous photograph.

1.1.1.3 Valley Sixty-fourths

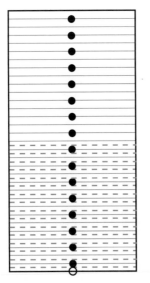
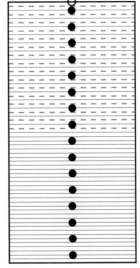

1.1.1.3_1
Begin by making the valley thirty-seconds. With a pencil, mark an X on each alternate crease. There will be 16 new Xs. Perhaps use a different colour or a different symbol to distinguish these marks from previous ones.

1.1.1.3_2
Fold the ○ edge to each X crease, marked here with a ●. There will be 16 new folds.

1.1.1.3_3
Repeat with the other edge, creating 16 more new folds.

1.1.1.3_4
This is the completed division of the paper into linear sixty-fourths. By repeating the system of marking each alternate fold and folding each edge in turn to those folds, the paper can be further divided into 128, 256 … and even more!

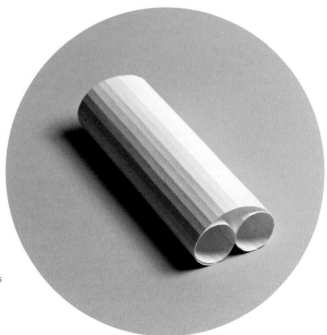

The paper is divided into sixty-fourths, using valley folds only. The result is a curled cylinder, not a pleat.

1.1.2 Dividing into Valley-Mountain Pleats

The previous exercises introduced the basic method of dividing paper. Using this knowledge, it is now possible to create valley-mountain pleats.

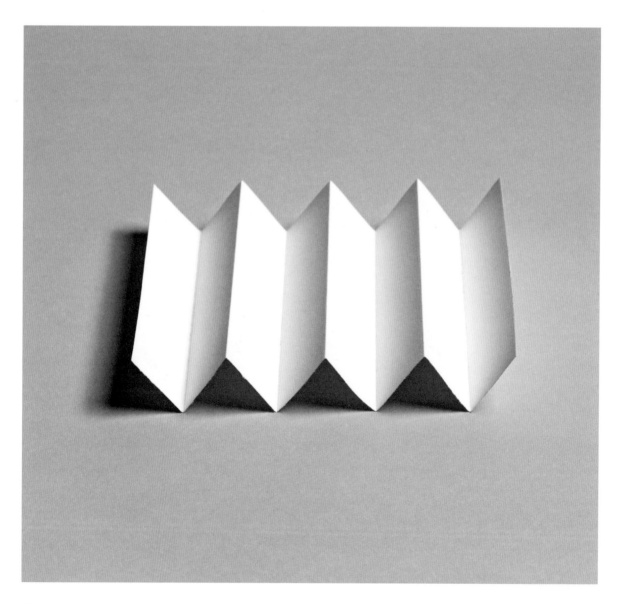

1.1.2.1 Pleated Eighths

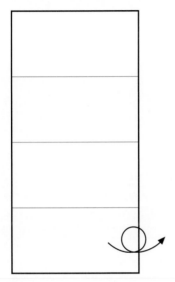

1.1.2.1_1
Follow the method of creating valley sixteenths (see page 24), but stop after Step 2, when the paper has been divided into valley quarters. Turn the paper over.

1.1.2.1_2
The existing folds are now mountain folds. Create a new valley fold by folding the ○ edge to the ● crease. Unfold.

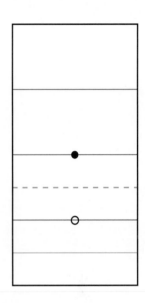

1.1.2.1_3
Create a new valley fold by folding the ○ mountain to lie on top of the ● mountain. Unfold.

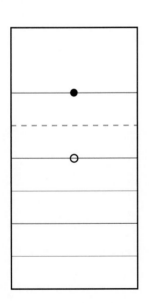

1.1.2.1_4
Similarly, create a new valley fold by folding the ○ mountain to lie on top of the ● mountain. Unfold. This step is simply a repeat of the previous step, but one division further up the paper.

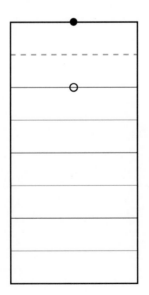

1.1.2.1_5
Finally, create a new valley fold by folding the ○ mountain to lie on top of the ● edge. Unfold.

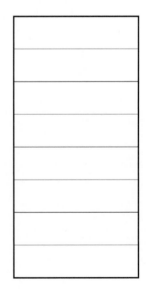

1.1.2.1_6
The paper is now pleated into eighths.

1.1.2.2 Pleated Sixteenths

1.1.2.2_1
Follow the method of creating valley sixteenths (see page 24), but stop after Step 6, when the paper has been divided into valley eighths.

1.1.2.2_2
Turn the paper over.

1.1.2.2_3
The existing folds are now mountain folds. Create a new valley fold by folding the ○ edge to the ● crease. Unfold.

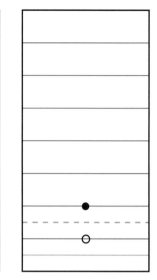

1.1.2.2_4
Create a new valley fold by folding the ○ mountain to lie on top of the ● mountain. Unfold.

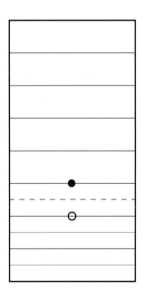

1.1.2.2_5
Similarly, create a new valley fold by folding the ○ mountain to lie on top of the ● mountain. Unfold. This step is simply a repeat of the previous step, but one division further up the paper.

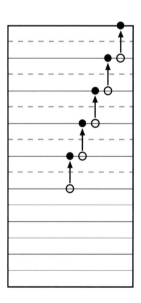

1.1.2.2_6
Repeat the process of placing a mountain fold on top of the mountain fold above it a further five more times. This will create a new valley fold between each existing mountain fold.

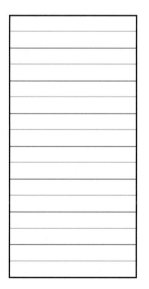

1.1.2.2_7
The paper is now pleated into sixteenths.

1.1.2.3   Pleated Thirty-seconds

1.1.2.3_1
Follow the method of creating valley sixteenths (see page 24), all the way to the end. Turn over.

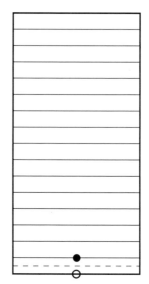

1.1.2.3_2
The existing creases are now all mountain folds.

1.1.2.3_3
Create a new valley fold by folding the ○ edge to the ● crease. Unfold.

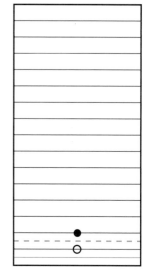

1.1.2.3_4
Create a new valley fold by folding the ○ mountain to lie on top of the ● mountain. Unfold.

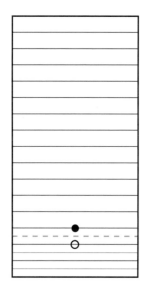

1.1.2.3_5
Similarly, create a new valley fold by folding the ○ mountain to lie on top of the ● mountain. Unfold. This step is simply a repeat of the previous step, but one division further up the paper.

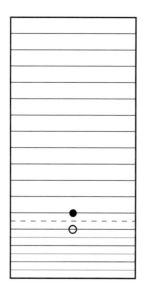

1.1.2.3_6
Again, create a new valley fold by folding the ○ mountain to lie on top of the ● mountain. Unfold. This step is a repeat of the previous step, but one division further up the paper.

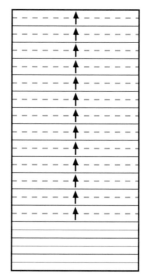

1.1.2.3_7
Repeat the process of placing a mountain fold on to the mountain fold above it 13 more times. This will create a new valley fold between each existing mountain fold.

1.1.2.3_8
The paper is now pleated into thirty-seconds.

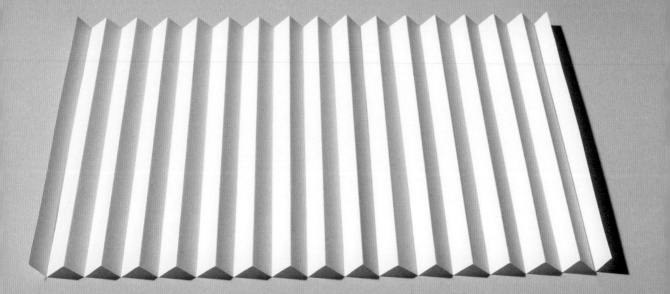

1.1.2.4 Pleated Sixty-fourths

1.1.2.4_1
Follow the method for creating valley thirty-seconds (see page 26) all the way to the end. Turn the paper over.

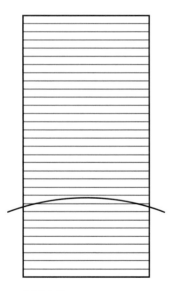

1.1.2.4_2
The existing folds are now mountain folds. The next step shows a close-up.

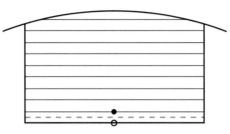

1.1.2.4_3
Create a new valley fold by folding the ○ edge to the ● crease. Unfold.

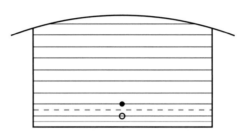

1.1.2.4_4
Create a new valley fold by folding the ○ mountain to lie on top of the ● mountain. Unfold.

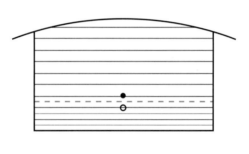

1.1.2.4_5
Repeat the process of placing a mountain fold on to the mountain fold above it 29 more times. This will create a new valley fold between each existing mountain fold.

1.1.2.4_6
The paper is now pleated into sixty-fourths.

1.1.3 Diagonal Divisions	All the previous examples have divided the paper from edge to edge, so that all the folds, whether valley or mountain, are parallel to the edges that create the first and last divisions.

However, it is also possible to partition the paper from corner to corner, dividing it along a diagonal. This simple idea permits many more pleated forms and surfaces to be created using the same technique of dividing as described above. |

1.1.3.1 The Basic Technique

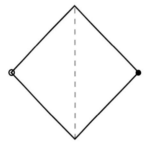

1.1.3.1_1
Begin with a square. Fold the left-hand ○ corner over to the right-hand ● corner. Open the paper.

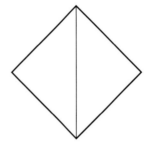

1.1.3.1_2
This crease line has no function in the final pleated structure, but it helps to locate all the folds that follow.

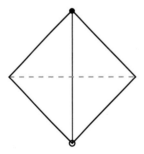

1.1.3.1_3
Fold the bottom ○ corner to the top ● corner. Open the paper.

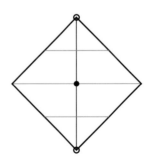

1.1.3.1_4
Divide into horizontal quarters by folding the ○ corners to the ● in the middle of the paper.

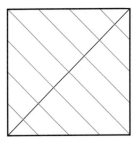 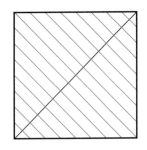 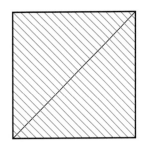 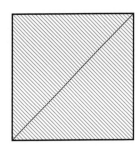

1.1.3.1_5
Use the technique described in 'Dividing into
Valleys Only' (see page 24) to divide the
paper into 8, 16, 32 or 64, along a diagonal.

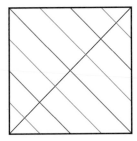 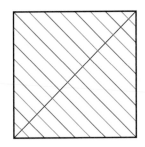 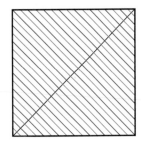 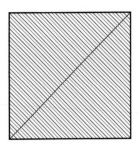

1.1.3.1_6
Use the technique described in 'Dividing
into Valley-Mountain Pleats' (see page 28)
to divide the paper into 8, 16, 32 or 64 pleats,
along a diagonal.

1.2
Rotational Divisions

Whereas linear divisions partition a *length*, rotational divisions partition an *angle*. The examples that follow are constructed in exactly the same way as the linear divisions described above, but can look very different.

Rotational Division

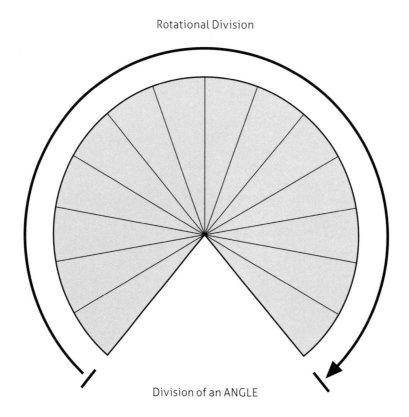

Division of an ANGLE

1.2_1
A rotational division partitions an angle into equal segments that progress from one end of the material to the opposite end. The angle can be any number of degrees (including greater than 360 degrees), and it can be divided into any number of equal segments.

1.2.1   Dividing into Valleys Only

This section is an abridgement of the same section in Linear Divisions above (see page 23). You are advised to have made the examples in the earlier section before attempting the ones described here.

1.2.1.1   Valley Eighths

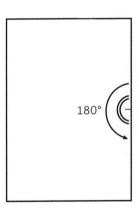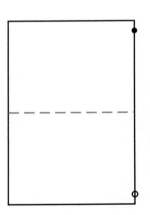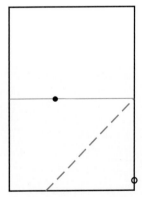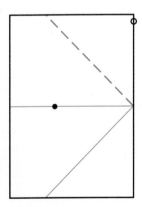

1.2.1.1_1
The angle to be divided is 180 degrees. It is seemingly invisible along the straight edge of the paper.

1.2.1.1_2
Fold the ○ end of the 180-degree arc to lie on the ● end. This will divide the angle in half, creating two angles of 90 degrees.

1.2.1.1_3
To next create angles which divide 180 degrees into quarters (each angle will be 45 degrees), fold the ○ edge to the ● crease.

1.2.1.1_4
Repeat Step 3 on the top half. This will divide 180 degrees into four angles of 45 degrees.

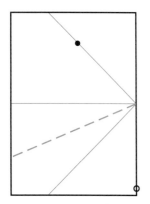

1.2.1.1_5
Bring the lower end of the
180-degree arc to the upper
quarter crease. Crease and unfold.

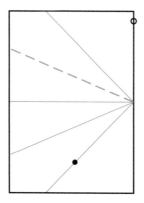

1.2.1.1_6
Similarly, bring the upper end
of the 180-degree arc to the
lower quarter crease. Crease
and unfold.

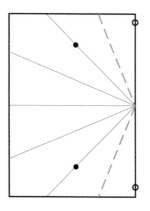

1.2.1.1_7
Bring each end of the 180-degree
arc to the nearer quarter crease.
Crease and unfold.

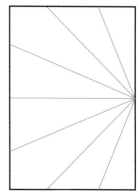

1.2.1.1_8
The 180-degree arc is now
divided into eight equal angles,
separated by valley folds. Note
how the method of construction
is exactly the same as for the
linear division.

1.2.1.2   Valley Sixteenths

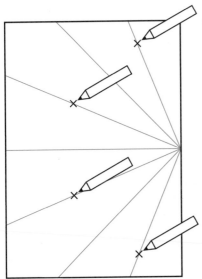

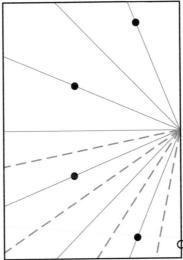

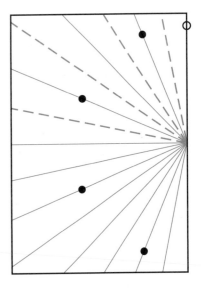

1.2.1.2_1
Begin by making the valley eighths, as previously. Mark each alternate crease with an X.

1.2.1.2_2
Bring the lower end of the 180-degree arc to each of the marked creases, creating four new valley folds. Repeat this with the upper end, creating four additional creases.

1.2.1.2_3
The 180-degree arc is now divided into 16 equal angles, separated by valley folds. Note how the method of construction is exactly the same as for the linear division.

1.2.2   Dividing into Valley-Mountain Pleats

Creating rotational valley-mountain pleats uses exactly the same method as the linear divisions, described on pages 30–37.

The example below shows how an angle of rotation of 180 degrees can be divided into 16 equal angles as a valley-mountain pleat. Refer to the linear division section to learn how a length can be divided into 32 or 64 pleats and extrapolate the method for rotational pleats.

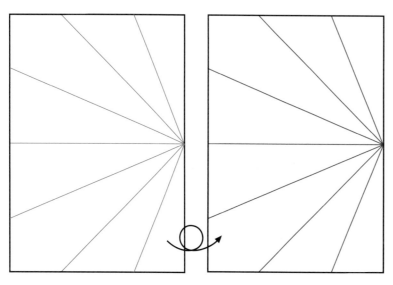

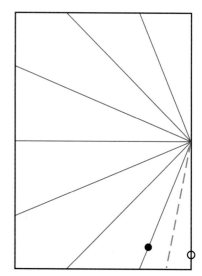

1.2.2_1
This is the arc of 180 degrees made in the previous section. All the folds are valleys. Turn over.

1.2.2_2
All the folds are now mountains.

1.2.2_3
Fold the lower end of the 180-degree arc to lie on top of the first mountain fold. Unfold.

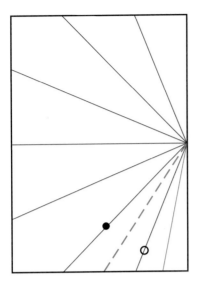

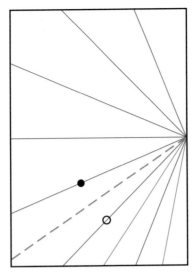

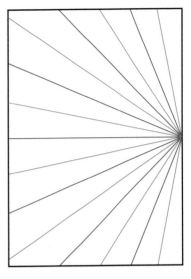

1.2.2_4
Lay the first mountain fold on top of the
second mountain fold, creating a valley fold
between them. Unfold.

1.2.2_5
Similarly, lay the second mountain fold
on top of the third, creating a valley fold
between them. Unfold.

1.2.2_6
Continue the sequence of laying each
mountain on top of the next, unfolding
each time, until the arc is fully pleated.
The arc of 180 degrees is now pleated into
16 equal angles.

1.2.3   Different Angles

When making linear pleats, a length is a length, whether it is 3 millimetres or 300 metres. The shape of the material will always look fundamentally the same – just longer or shorter – and the pleats will always make a regular corrugation.

However, when making rotational pleats, the shape of the paper can look radically different, depending on the angle of rotation that has been chosen, the number of divisions created and how the material is cut to its final shape.

For these reasons, rotational pleats may be considered to have a greater versatility of design than the better-known linear pleats.

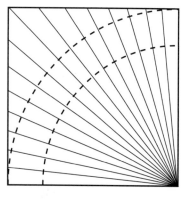 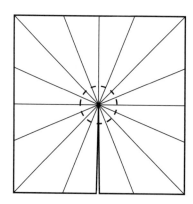 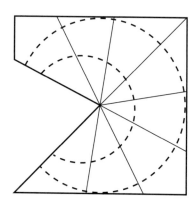

1.2.3_1
Here, three examples show some of the many possibilities when folding and cutting rotational pleats. It is possible to create angles greater than 360 degrees by gluing pieces together to resemble pencil shavings (correctly known as a 'helix'). In this way, it is possible to construct and pleat angles from many hundreds or even thousands of degrees of paper or another material.

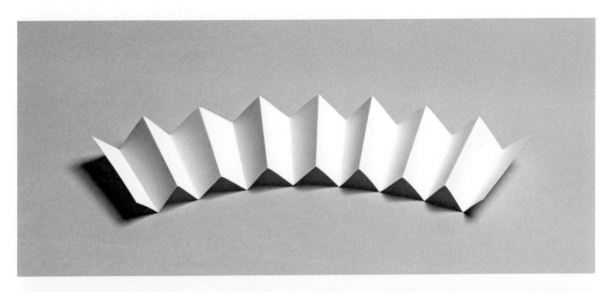

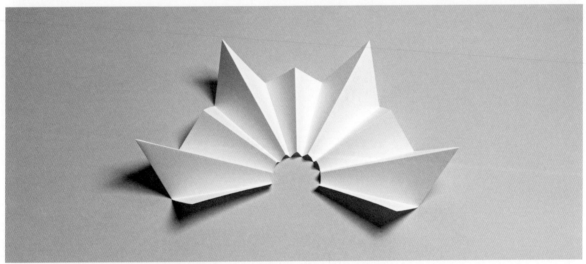

1.3
Grids

A grid is made when one line of pleats is superimposed on top of another line, but at a different rotation. There are many ways in which this can occur, but grids take two fundamentally different forms: grids with lines of pleats rotated at 45 or 90 degrees to each other, and grids where the pleats are rotated at 60 or 120 degrees to each other. The construction of both of these sets is described here.

1.3.1 Ninety-degree Grids

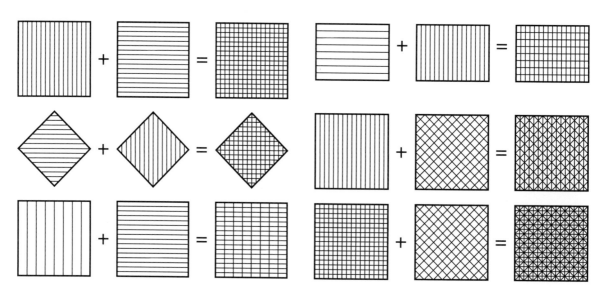

1.3.1_1

Here are six ways in which between two and four lines of pleats can be superimposed at 45 or 90 degrees to each other. What they have in common is that they are all placed on a rectangle of material (a square is a special kind of rectangle). Each line of pleats is made following the methods described previously in the chapter. Whether the material is divided into 8, 16, 32, 64 ... or whatever, is entirely at the discretion of the designer.

Grids have a near-infinite number of uses, some of which will be explored later in this book.

1.3.2   Sixty-degree Grids

Sixty-degree grids are much less commonly made
than their 90-degree cousins, doubtless because
they are more intricate to construct and because they
create lesser-used triangles and hexagons, rather than
rectangles. Nevertheless, they are hugely interesting,
and any serious student of pleating should explore
them deeply.

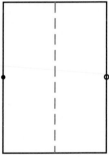

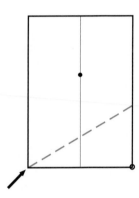

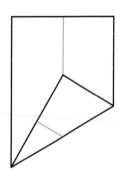

1.3.2_1
Begin with a rectangle of A3 or A4 paper
(11¾ x 16½ or 8 x 11¾in). Fold it in half down
the centre. Unfold.

1.3.2_2
This next fold is a particularly beautiful piece
of origami geometry, which never fails to
delight. Place the ○ corner at the bottom right
of the rectangle on to the centre line at ●,
such that the new fold begins exactly at the
bottom left-hand corner.

1.3.2_3
This is the result. Open the fold.

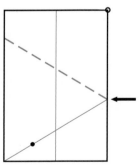

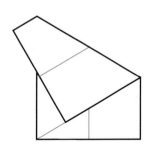

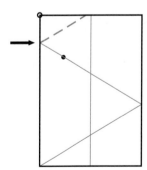

1.3.2_4
Place the ○ corner on the new fold line at
● so that both folds exactly meet at the
arrowed point.

1.3.2_5
This is the result. Open the fold.

1.3.2_6
Similarly, place the ○ corner on the new fold
line at ●, so that both folds exactly meet at
the arrowed point. Open the fold.

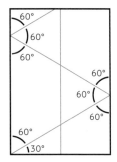

1.3.2_7
A brief analysis of the folding pattern is instructive. The fold made in Step 2 created angles of 60 and 30 degrees at the bottom right-hand corner of the rectangle, which then permitted the creation of multiple 60-degree angles on the right- and left-hand edges. It is remarkable how simply this tri-section is achieved!

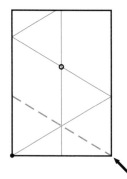

1.3.2_8
Steps 2 to 6 are now repeated, but this time beginning by folding the bottom left-hand corner to the centre line. This creates a mirror image of Step 2.

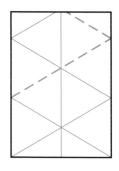

1.3.2_9
Follow Steps 3 to 6, thereby creating two more folds that mirror the existing folds.

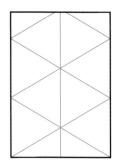

1.3.2_10
This is the first – and simplest – grid of folds. Note how the paper is divided into equilateral triangles, with angles of 60 degrees. The folding that now follows divides and subdivides the triangles, making the grid ever more dense.

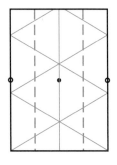

1.3.2_11
Bring the edges to the centre line. Unfold.

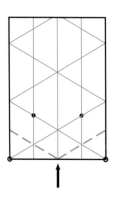

1.3.2_12
Make two new folds, as shown. Each is the mirror of the other. Note how the ○ corners are placed on the ● intersections, and both folds exactly meet at the arrowed point on the bottom edge. Be accurate.

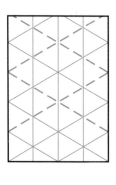

1.3.2_13
Using the Step 12 folds as a guide, repeat the method described in Steps 4 to 8 to create a series of zigzag folds that progress up the sheet. Note how a grid of equal-sized equilateral triangles is created.

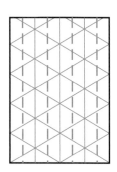

1.3.2_14
Create more verticals that divide the width of the rectangle into eight. The method for dividing into eight is described in 'Dividing into Valleys Only' (see page 24).

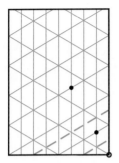

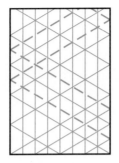

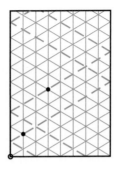

1.3.2_15
Fold the ○ corner to both of the
● intersections to create two
new folds.

1.3.2_16
Using both of the Step 15 folds
as a guide, repeat the method
described in Steps 4 and 8 to
create two series of zigzag folds
that progress up the sheet.

1.3.2_17
Fold the ○ corner to both of the
● intersections to create two
new folds, then use those folds
to repeat Step 16, creating two
new series of zigzags that
progress up the sheet.

1.3.2_18
This is the final grid. The paper
is divided into eight across
its width, so the grid can be
described as a grid of equilateral
triangles, divided into eight. The
grid can be further subdivided
into 16 and 32, using the method
described here, but at ever
smaller iterations.

If you wish this grid to be not all
valleys, but a valley-mountain
pleat, simply turn over after Step
13 and continue as instructed.

1.3.2_19
An interesting variation is to
create the grid on a hexagon, not
a rectangle. Since the hexagon
already has angles of 120 and
60 degrees, it is not necessary
to create these angles in Step 2.
Instead, simply create three
lines of parallel folds, dividing
the hexagon into 8, 16, 32, 64 …
or whatever, across its width, as
described earlier in the chapter.

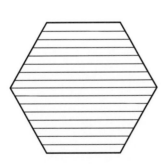

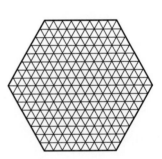

1.3.2_20
To make a hexagon, proceed to
Step 13 and cut a large hexagon
from the rectangle. For beginners,
it is better to start with
larger rectangles, such as A3 or A2
(16½ x 23½in), than with A4,
particularly when dividing the
paper into dense grids.

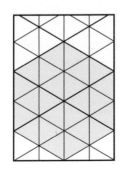

49

1.4
Graphic Divisions

The low-tech, handmade methods of dividing paper described in this chapter will work for anyone, anywhere, at any reasonable scale. Folded well, they are very accurate and do away with the need to use equipment or technology of any sort.

Nevertheless, there may be times when dividing the paper manually will not work well, in which case, one of the two methods described below will be a good substitute.

Using a Ruler and Pencil

Not everything can be neatly designed to have exactly 2, 4, 8, 16, 32 or 64 divisions as described in this chapter. There may be occasions when you need to divide an awkward length by an awkward number of divisions. But how?

Imagine then, that you need to divide a length of 773mm into 14 identical divisions. That's 55.214mm per division. It's not the simplest distance to measure 14 times, one after another in a straight line, but with care, it is certainly possible and should not be beyond the capabilities of a designer-maker. In any case, there is no other way, other than the high-tech method described in the 'Using CAD' section (opposite). So, if a ruler and pencil really is the best method for measuring, use it.

Consider first marking or folding the distances not on the material itself, but on a length of till tape, then transferring the measurements to the final material. (Till tape is the roll of paper tape used in cash registers.) In this way you will have a permanent and reusable template. Since till tape is many metres long, it also permits the option of measuring large distances.

A trick to avoid most of the measuring is to add two extra divisions of 55.214mm to the 14 needed, to create a new total length of 16 x 55.214mm. Measure the material (or a length of till tape) to be the same length. It is then a simple matter to fold it into

16 divisions by the method described in 'Valley Sixteenths' (see page 24) and then – here's the clever part – to remove two divisions at the end. Nice! Of course, it is not always practical to 'round up' the number of divisions to 4, 8, 16, 32 or 64 and then remove the excess, but when feasible, it's a great time saver.

A ruler and pencil will also be useful to measure incremental pleats (see 'Incremental Accordion Pleats' on page 61) and any pleat pattern where the divisions are irregular.

Using CAD

Another way to construct divisions or a pleat pattern is to use CAD software to create an accurate drawing of what you wish to make, then to print it out at 1:1 scale using a computer printer or, for larger images, a plotter. The printed lines can then be folded along to create a very accurate, full-size maquette. In some cases, the ink will weaken the paper sufficiently to enable you to fold along the inked crease lines with surprising ease.

This method, though initially potentially time-consuming, is an excellent way to test a pattern before making it in something more permanent or more expensive. Its added advantage over the ruler and pencil method is that multiple copies can be created and adaptations can be incorporated easily.

If you have access to a plotter that can cut and score the material (not necessarily paper), or even have access to a laser cutter, these methods are the ultimate in quick, accurate prototyping.

2

BASIC PLEATS

Basic Pleats

This chapter is the technical heart of the book. It describes in detail the characteristics and uses of all the basic pleat patterns – how they relate to each other, how they differ and how they evolve from the simple accordion pleat.

Some of the pleats will probably be familiar to you. Who among us has not seen an accordion or knife pleat, used countless times in apparel, around the home and even in architecture. However, this book contextualizes them and shows many variations that will be unfamiliar to all but the most dedicated pleater.

The book also introduces basic but perhaps unfamiliar pleating patterns. They are just as useful as the more familiar patterns, but being less familiar, they are also more innovative and exciting to use.

You are advised to work through this chapter, making as many of the basic examples as you can, then labelling and filing them for use later. There is nothing better than having something in the hand to play with, twist, bend, open and mangle for generating ideas when working on a project or brief.

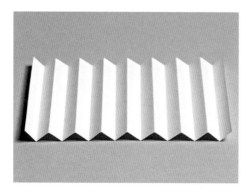
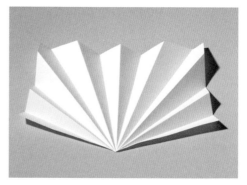

2.1
Accordion Pleats

A chapter entitled 'Basic Pleats' must start with accordion pleats. These are the simplest and most common of all pleats, so ubiquitous they are almost invisible. They are popular for good reason: accordion pleats are functional, immensely versatile and are quick and easy to make in almost any material.

This section describes their basic structure and offers many suggestions for how to give their familiar zigzag surface a creative twist.

2.1.1   Basic Examples

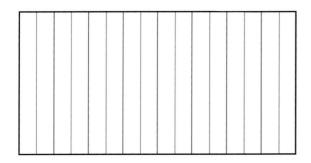

2.1.1_1
Here are the two basic forms of accordion pleats – the linear and the rotational. The linear example shows a span divided into equal lengths, and the rotational example shows an angle divided into smaller equal angles. For details of how they are constructed, see 'Pleated Sixteenths' for creating linear divisions (page 30) and 'Dividing into Valley-Mountain Pleats' (page 42) for creating rotational divisions.

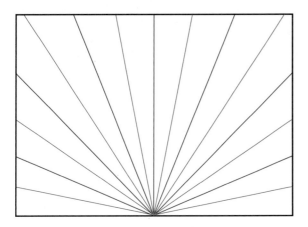

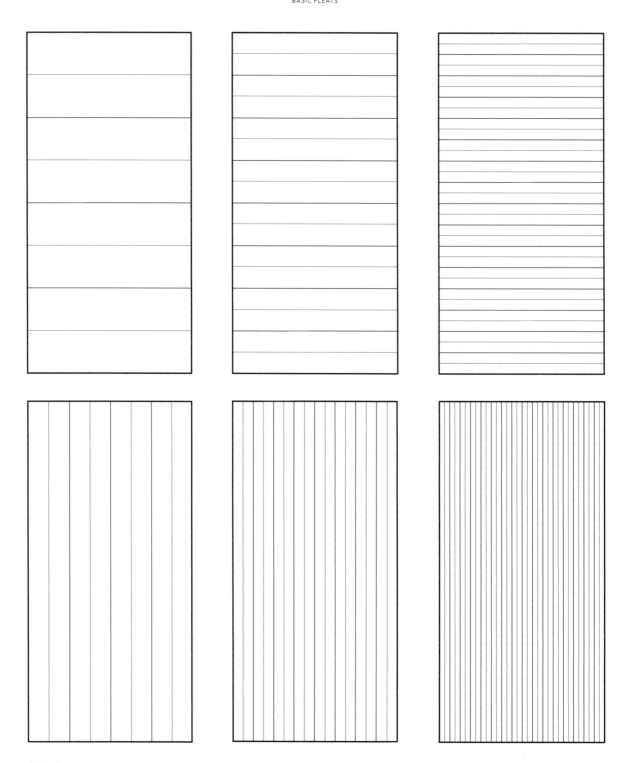

2.1.1_2
Linear accordion pleats can divide a length into any number of divisions, either horizontally or vertically. The examples here show pleats with 8, 16 and 32 divisions, made horizontally and vertically on rectangles of the same shape. Refer to the previous chapter (see pages 28 – 35) to learn how to divide the paper.

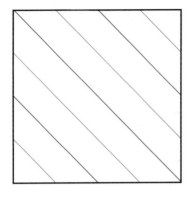 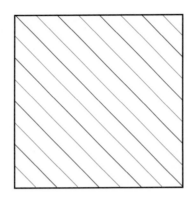

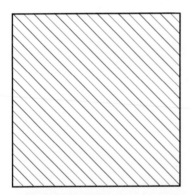 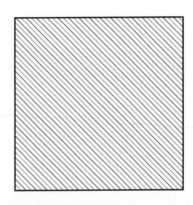

2.1.1_3
Similarly, the surface can be divided
diagonally into any number of equal divisions.
Refer to the previous chapter to learn how to
divide paper diagonally (see pages 36 – 37).

Above
Evenly spaced pine battens clad one side of a conventional concrete building in a redeveloped park and factory complex adjacent to the main Shanghai-Zhujiajiao highway in China. The delicately pleated façade gives a sense of privacy to the restaurant inside and also hides air-conditioning units. Designed by Scenic Architecture, Shanghai (China).

Right
The 'Zig-zag Chair' from 1934 is one of the most iconic designs of the twentieth century. It unites function with a minimalist pleated form to create an object that is uncompromisingly rational. Designed by Gerrit Rietveld (the Netherlands).

Left
The pleated wall is part of an installation in which an assembly of high-density concrete panels are embedded with optical fibres. Light shining on the panels from the back passes through the fibres to illuminate the reverse side like a screen. The fibres become dark when a shadow interrupts the light. Designed by Kengo Kuma, Tokyo (Japan).

2.1.1_4
Rotational accordion pleats can divide any
angle into any number of smaller, equal angles.
The method for creating rotational divisions
can be learnt in the previous chapter
(see pp 38 – 43).

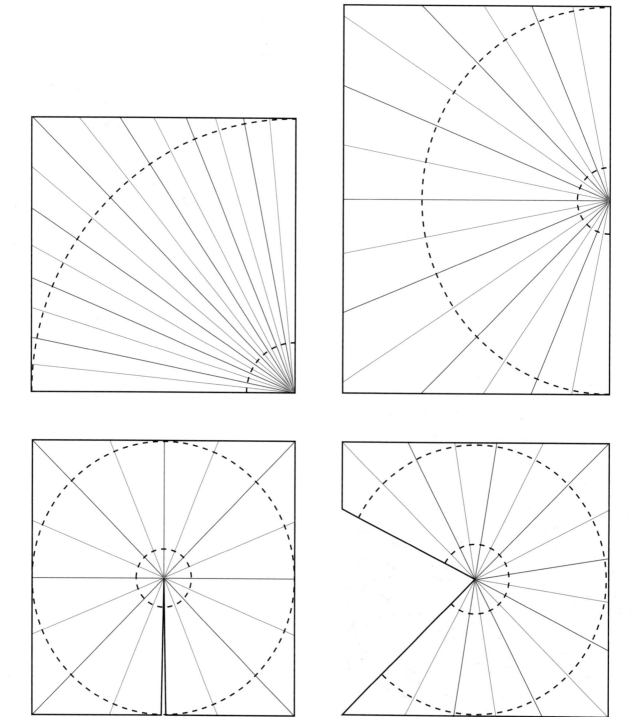

2.1.2 Incremental Accordion Pleats

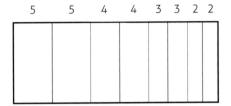

| 5 | 5 | 4 | 4 | 3 | 3 | 2 | 2 |

2.1.2_1
Accordion pleats can increase or decrease in size as they progress across a surface. In this example, adjacent pleats are proportioned 5, 4, 3 and 2, so that they stand stably on a surface.

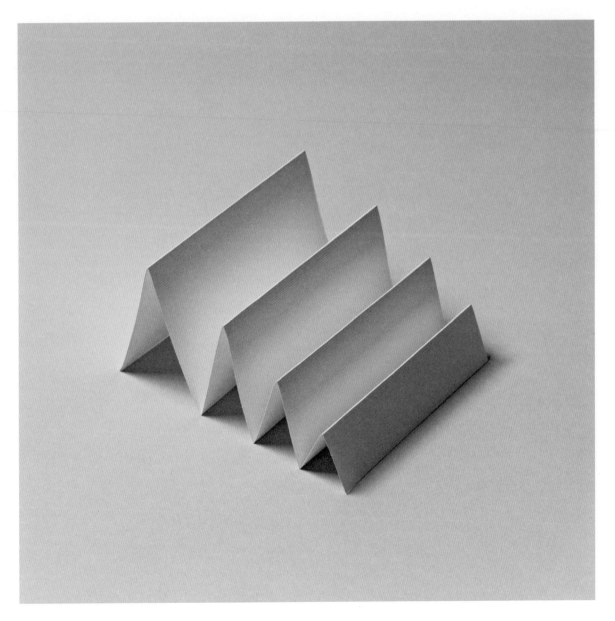

14	13	12	11	10	9	8	7	6	5	4	3

2.1.2_2
Instead of being grouped
in pairs, as in the previous example,
individual distances can also increase or
decrease incrementally, as shown here.

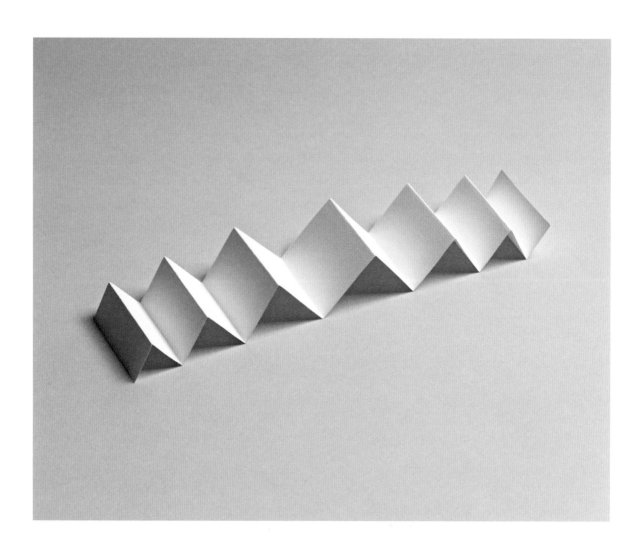

2.1.2_3
On extended strips, pleats can increase
and decrease. Incremental pleats can also
be made rotationally, increasing and
decreasing angles.

2.1.3   Rhythms

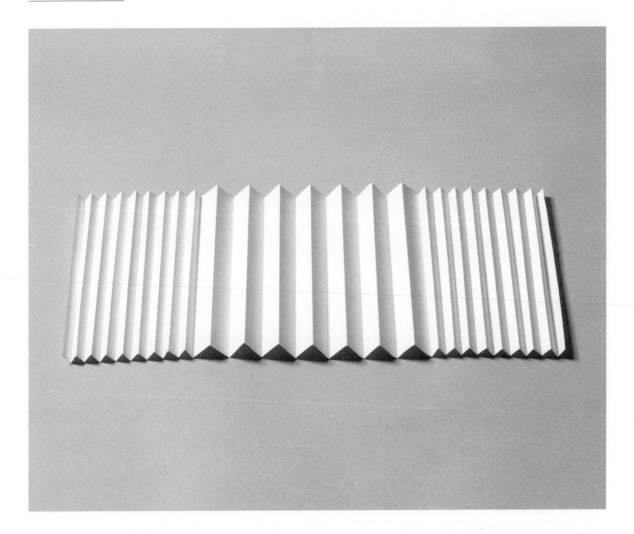

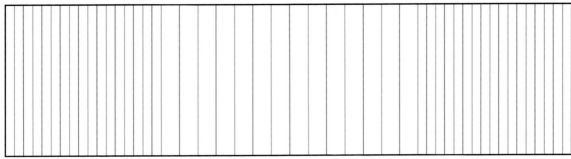

2.1.3_1
Pleats of the same size can be placed in a block,
then this can be placed adjacent to a block of
pleats that are larger or smaller, to create a
rhythm of alternating 'large-small' blocks.

2.1.3_2
Creating rhythmic patterns of accordion
pleats in different sizes is a simple pencil and
paper game. If you are experimenting
directly with paper, divide it into 32 or 64
before beginning, so that you have a large
number of divisions to play with (see 'Linear
Divisions', page 23).

Above
A series of accordion pleats of different
sizes were made in paper and overlaid on top
of each other, creating a series of repeat and
non-repeat shadow patterns. The shadows
were analyzed and re-interpreted as
a two-dimensional repeat textile print.
Designed by Elisheva Fineman. Student
project, Department of Textile Design,
Shenkar College, Tel Aviv (Israel).

2.1.4 Material Shape

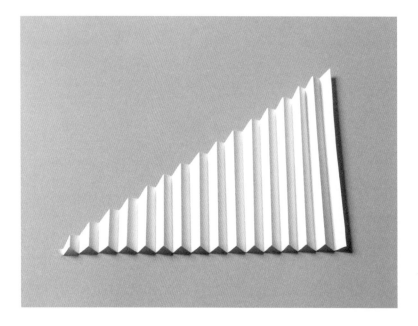

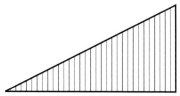

2.1.4_1
Conventional rectangles and circles offer many opportunities for experimenting with accordion pleats – or any other type of pleat – but if the shape of the material is changed, other possibilities arise, particularly in the relationship between the pleats and the edge(s) of the material.

In this example, the sloping edge of the triangle creates an appealing zigzag edge when the pleats are gathered up.

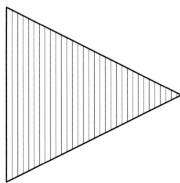

2.1.4_2
If the shape of the triangle is changed, the zigzag effect can be created on two edges.

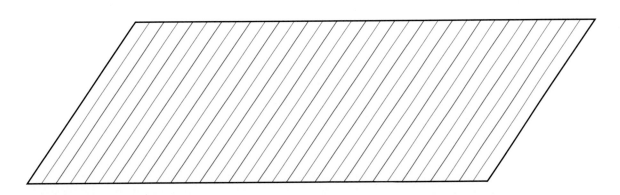

2.1.4_3
If the polygon is a parallelogram or rhombus
and the pleats are laid parallel to the sloping
edges, then the zigzag effect is created on
two edges, but one zigzag is on the front
side and one is on the reverse.

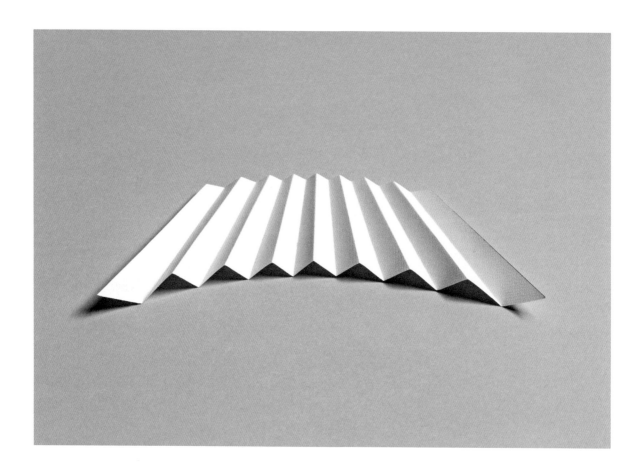

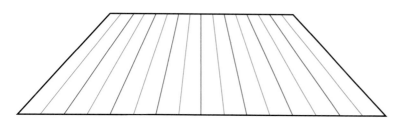

2.1.4_4
A rotational pleat need not be cut as an arc of
a circle. In this example, the pleats converge
at an imaginary point above the material, but
the polygon is a straight-sided trapezium.

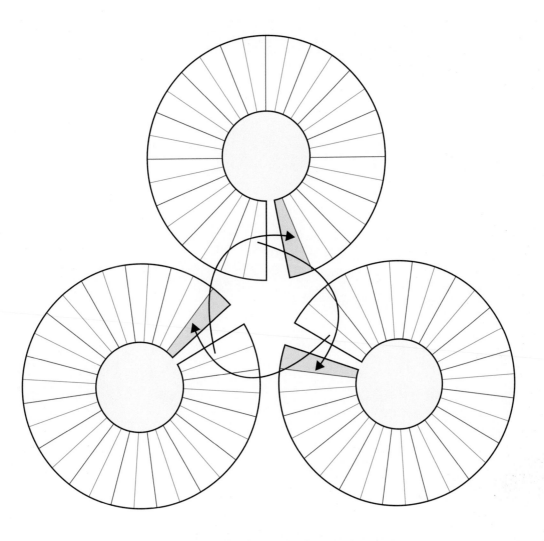

2.1.4_5
Rotational pleats need not be limited to 360 degrees. A succession of pleated circles can be joined together to create a dense surface of rotational pleats. In this example, three circles are joined together, but it could be many more.

A series of cuts ingeniously permit
a wooden surface to stretch open to
create a continuous line that resembles
the edge of an accordion pleat (see image
opposite). This linear concept of a pleat is
unique in the book. Designed by Randy
Weersing (USA).

2.1.5   Gathering and Spreading

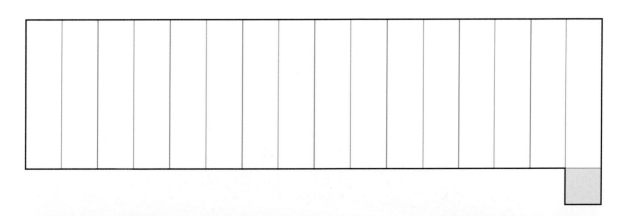

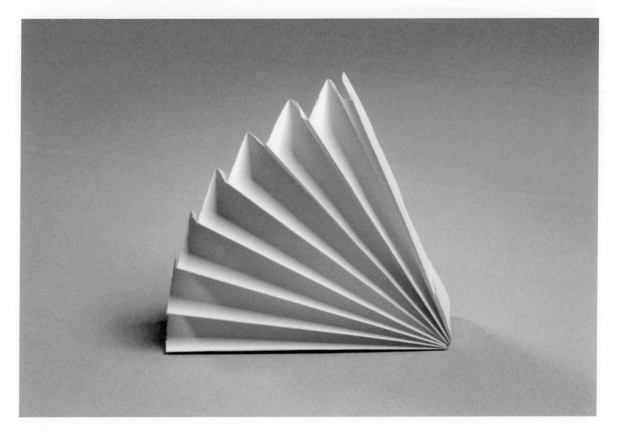

2.1.5_1

Any accordion pleat, whether linear or rotational, can be gathered together at one end (or both), permitting the rest of the material to spread open. The constriction and expansion offered by these – and most other – pleats offer exciting possibilities for new surfaces and forms.

In this example, the small glue tab holds all the pleats together to create a simple fan shape.

A long line of tiny accordion pleats are glued
into a cylinder and pushed flat to resemble
a circular fan, which then forms the basis
of this elegant 3D watch face. Designed by
Benjamin Hubert for Nava Design (UK/Italy).

2.1.5_2
By making small tabs that close each
individual pleat, the edge is not totally
closed, as seen in the previous example,
but only half closed.

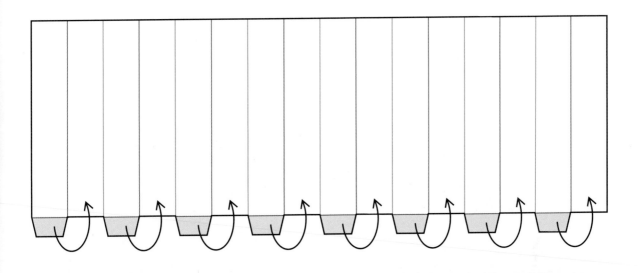

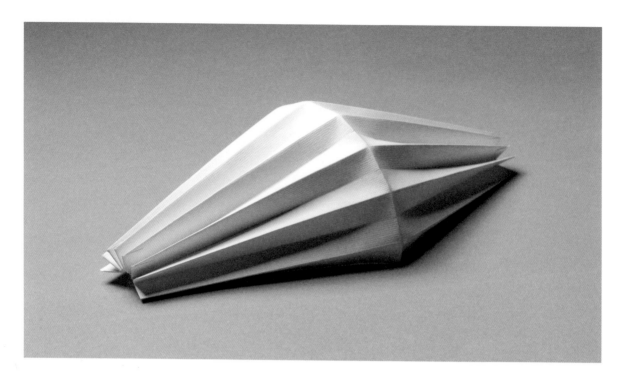

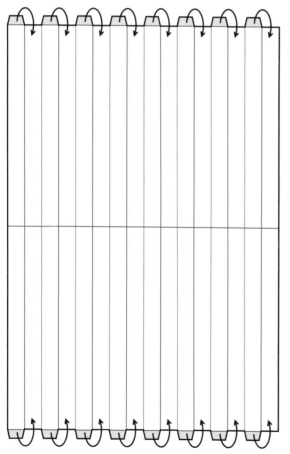

2.1.5_3
It is possible to gather both ends, allowing the single horizontal mountain fold to stretch the material open dramatically.

2.2

Knife Pleats

Knife pleats are close relatives of accordion pleats, but more decorative and perhaps also more useful because they can lie flat. This characteristic means that knife pleats are commonly used on the body, where a uniform body-hugging surface is often important.

2.2.1   Basic Examples

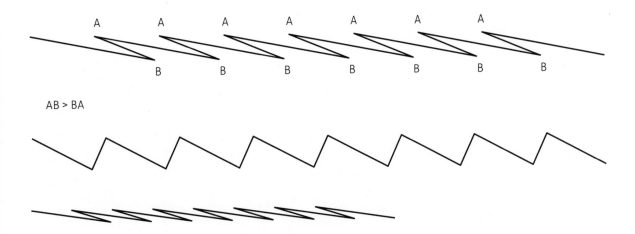

AB > BA

2.2.1_1
Like an accordion pleat, a knife pleat is the pairing of a mountain fold with a valley fold, but the difference is that the distances between the folds are not equal. The effect of this 'longer-shorter-longer-shorter...' pattern is to create a pleat that travels across a surface and which – unlike an accordion pleat – will lie flat.

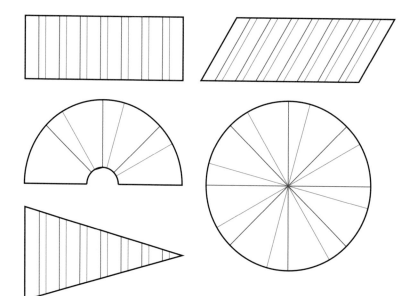

2.2.1_2
Knife pleats can be linear or rotational, and
laid across materials of different shapes.

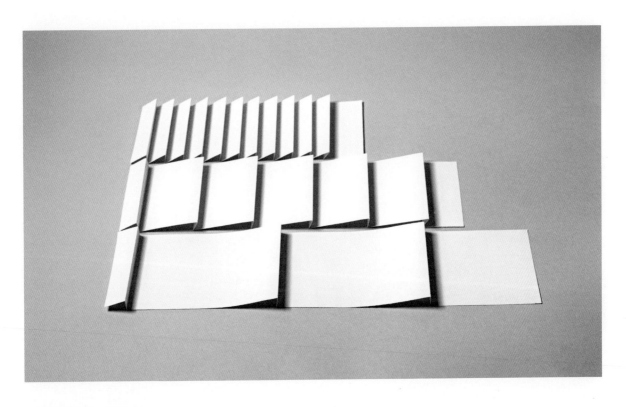

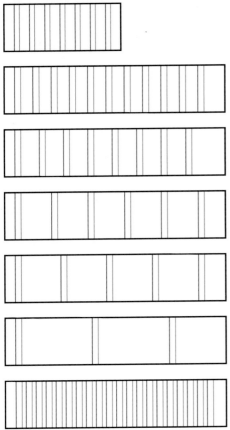

2.2.1_3
The 'longer-shorter-longer-shorter …' pattern that defines a knife pleat can be made in any proportion. In these examples, the distance between the mountain and the valley remains constant, but the distance between the valley and the mountain steadily increases, so that the pleats become increasingly separated from each other.

In the bottom illustration, the distance between the valley fold and the mountain fold to its right is less than the distance between the valley and the mountain to its left. This is in contrast to all the illustrations above it. The effect is still to create a Knife pleat, but the direction is reversed.

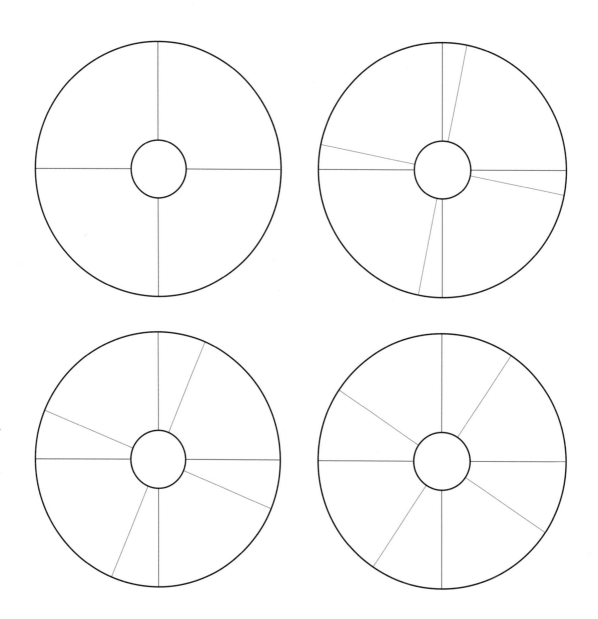

2.2.1_4
The same principle can also be applied
to rotational knife pleats.

Here, the top left-hand drawing shows four
mountain folds, which are repeated in the
other drawings. The angle between the
mountain and the valley increases from
drawing to drawing to create a series of
knife pleats of different proportions.

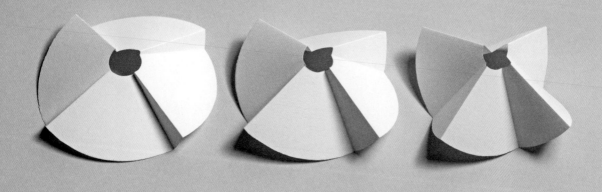

Above
This fantasy wedding gown and train makes extravagant use of layered knife pleats to create a look that is both sumptuous and feminine. As the wearer moves, the pleats ruffle and bounce to create a flurry of movement. Designed by Anthropologie (USA).

Opposite
Precisely made knife pleats allow the paper to open and gather to create complex curved surfaces reminiscent of an unspecified organic form. The lyricism and elegance of the structure belie its origin as a flat sheet of paper. Designed by Richard Sweeney (UK).

This monumental glass curtain wall features a line of thirteen irregular mountain/valley pleats along one elevation and five on an adjacent one, to a height of eight floors, creating dramatic shadows at all times of the day. Designed by J. J. Pan & Partners (Taiwan).

2.2.2   Reflections

2.2.2_1
A characteristic of knife pleats is that as they travel across a surface, they create a series of steps, much like a staircase.

Many new possibilities for surfaces and forms become possible if a line of knife pleats is reflected, so that the steps first ascend, then descend (or the opposite). In this linear example, the knife pleats ascend to a central platform, then descend.

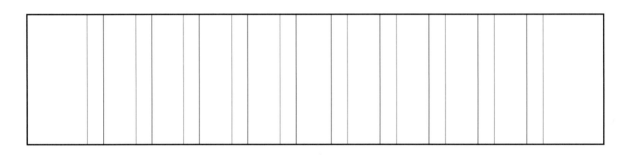

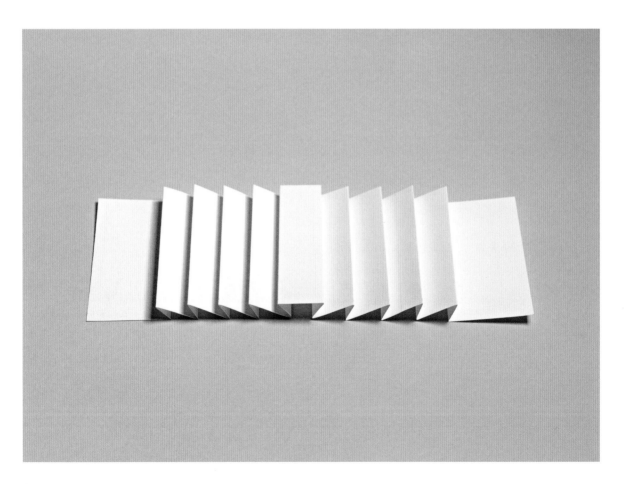

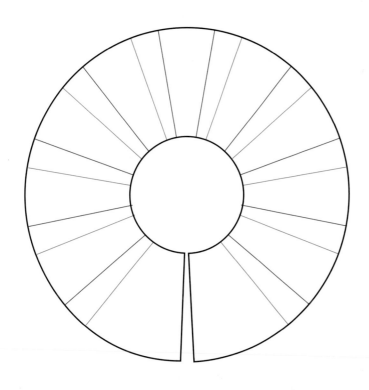

2.2.2_2
Similarly, a line of rotational knife pleats
ascends to a central platform, then descends.

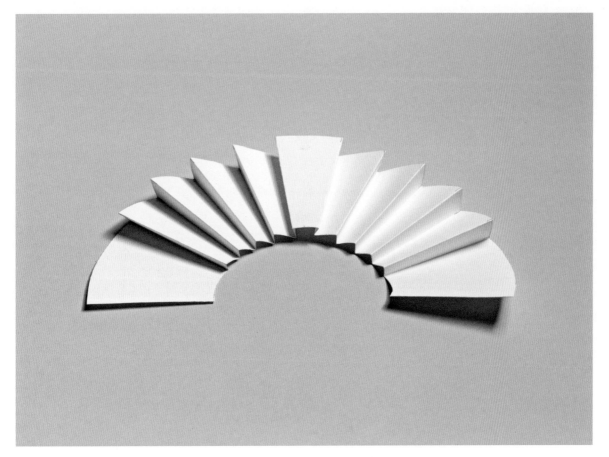

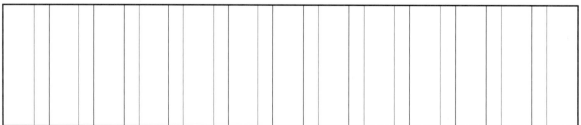

2.2.2_3
Ascending and descending knife pleats can be
created many times in many different patterns.

Sheets of marine plywood are cut to subtly different shapes, each resembling an upside-down letter 'L'. The pieces are placed side by side, with each one a little offset from its neighbours. The effect is to create a knife pleat, on both the inside and the outside surfaces. The result is a very subtle, visually complex object. Designed by Chris Hardy (USA).

2.2.3   Gathering and Spreading

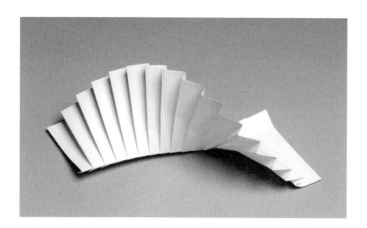

2.2.3_1
The ability of knife pleats to lie flat means that it is easy to gather them flat at one end, or at both ends. In this example, the line of knife pleats is made, then a long mountain fold is put in to gather one end, allowing the ungathered end to expand freely. The effect is to create a spiral. When using fabric, the long mountain would be substituted by a line of stitching.

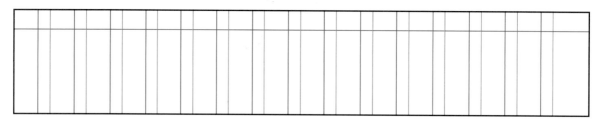

2.2.3_2
When the long mountain is placed in the centre, the pleats step away symmetrically from the centre line.

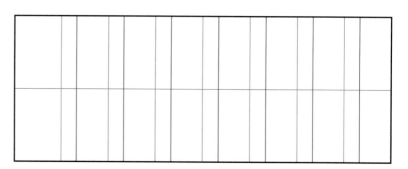

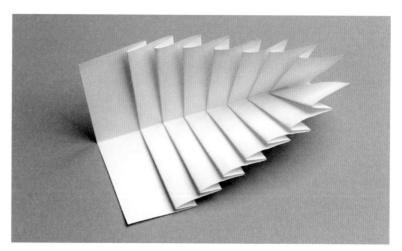

2.2.3_3
Here, the pattern of folds seen in the previous example is mirrored, so that the pleats step away from each other towards the centre and then close up again as they process towards the other side.

The 'opening-closing' pattern could be endlessly repeated down a long strip.

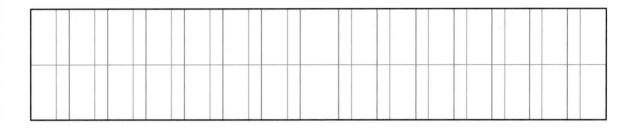

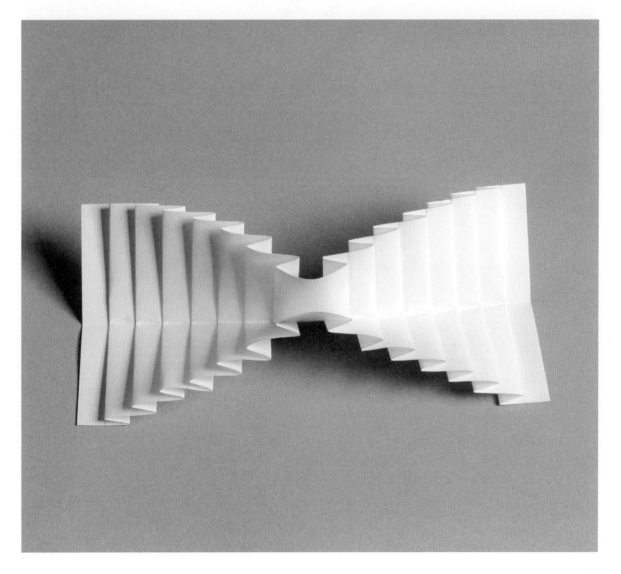

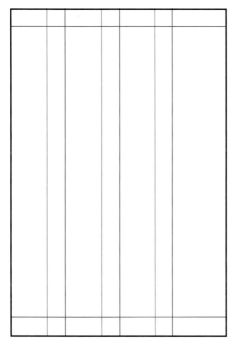

2.2.3_4
Both ends of a line of knife pleats can be
gathered flat with horizontal mountain folds.
When held securely, the centre of the pleats
can be pulled open, expanding the surface.

Opposite
This delicate paper vase was folded in a
series of knife pleats gathered together
at the narrow neck. Although pleasingly
hand-made in appearance, the crease pattern
is very precise. The use of acrylic colour
and the torn edge add greatly to its appeal.
Height: 20cm (8in). Designed by Rebecca
Gieseking (USA).

2.3

Box Pleats

Box pleats are similar to knife pleats, ideal for use on the body, or anywhere where a flat but structurally stable, decorative surface is needed. They are the sensible, easy-going member of the pleat family.

2.3.1   Basic Examples

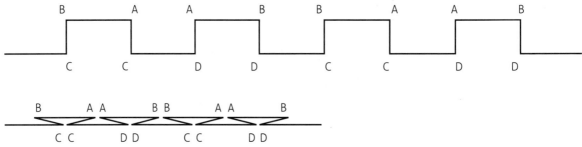

2.3.1_1
The accordion and knife pleats described previously have a simple two-fold cycle of repeats; one mountain fold is followed by one valley fold, then the cycle repeats.

Box pleats, however, have a four-fold cycle of repeats: 'valley-mountain-mountain-valley …'. They can be pulled open to resemble boxes, or flattened. When flat, they resemble knife pleats, but whereas a line of knife pleats creates a line of steps, a line of box pleats remains flat and is identical front and back. For this reason, although pleasingly decorative, they are also relatively undynamic.

2.3.1_2
This is the classic pattern
of linear box pleats.

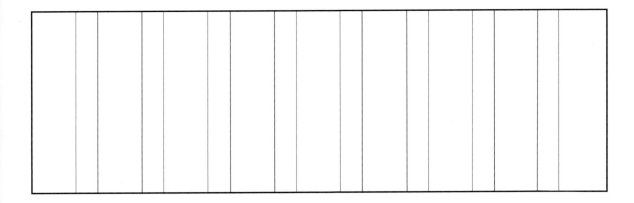

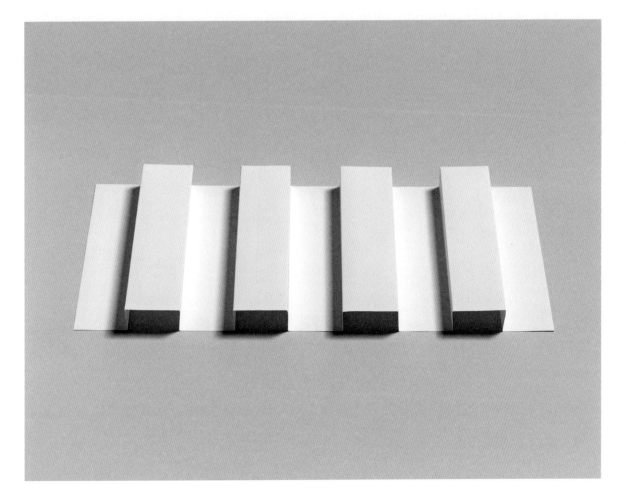

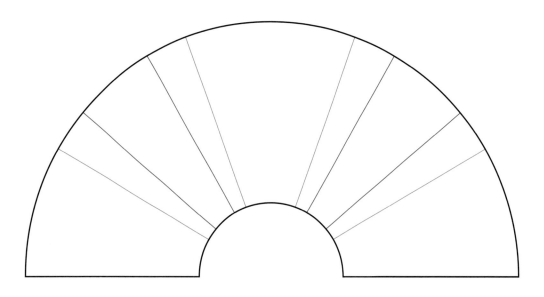

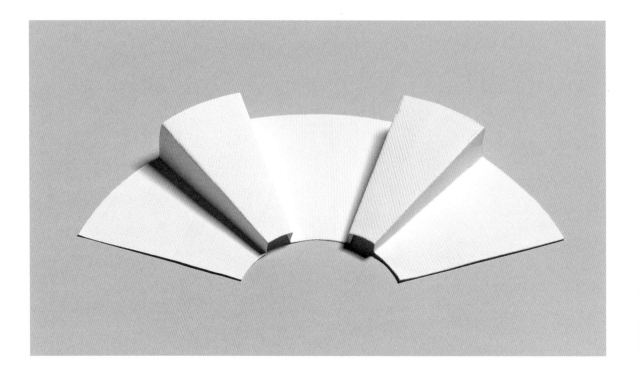

2.3.1_3
Here, two box pleats are placed in a
rotational configuration.

This page and overleaf
Thousands of sheets, or wide strips, of
brown kraft paper (above) or polyethylene
(overleaf) are intermittently glued together
so that, when stretched apart, they create
a honeycomb effect of box pleats. The
designers have used this construction
method to create a wide variety of seating,
lighting, and wall barriers. Designed by
Molo (Canada).

2.3.2 Advanced Examples

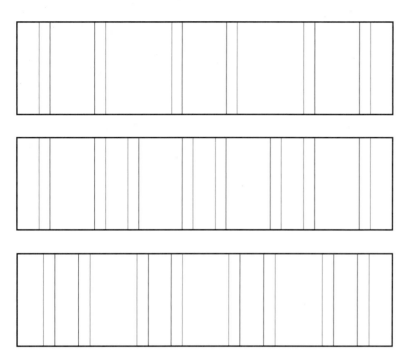

2.3.2_1
With four folds in the box pleat cycle, there are many more possibilities for rhythmic variations than with the simpler two-fold cycle of accordion or knife pleats. Here are three linear examples, but there are many more options.

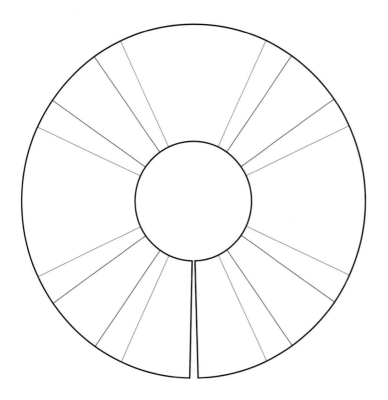

2.3.2_2
There are likewise many rotational
variations. Here is just one.

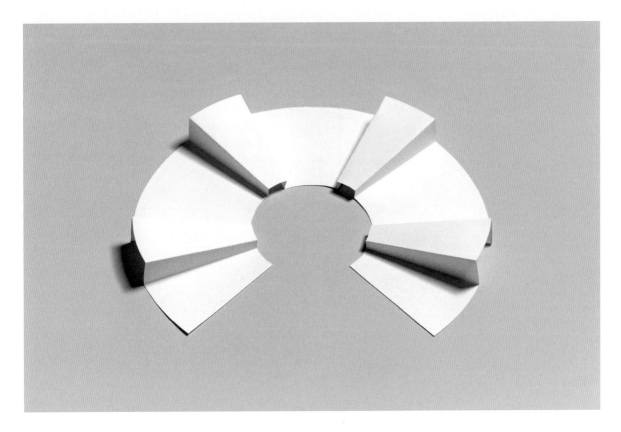

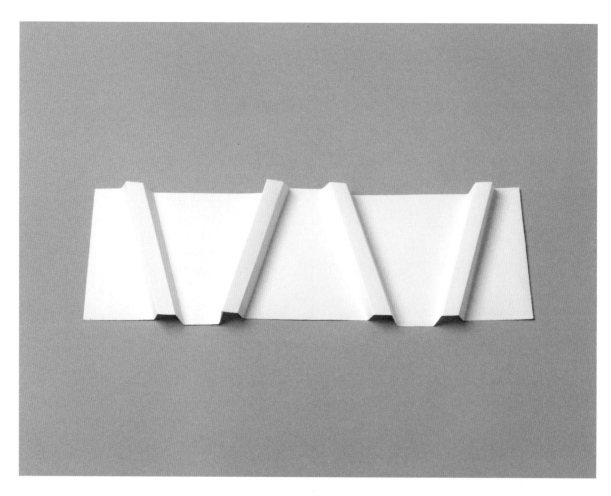

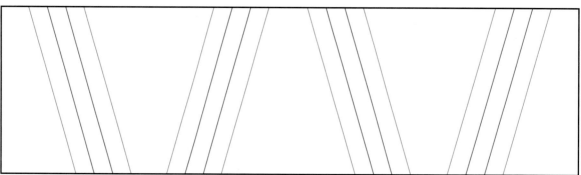

2.3.2_3
Box pleats can be placed individually at an
angle on a sheet of material, to create an
interesting interplay between the raised
'box' and the flat surface beneath.

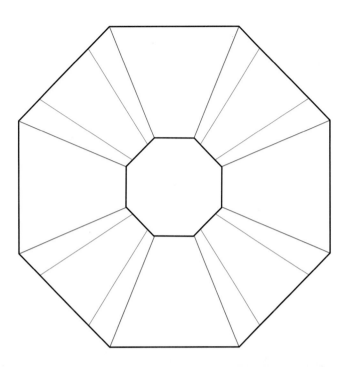

2.3.2_4
When added to a regular polygon – in this
example an octagon – many funnel-like
forms can be created. The two examples
show the front and back surfaces.

2.3.2_5
The placement of two box pleats that meet at the corner of a void can create the illusion of a complex solid form. The folding pattern is simple, but the result is pleasingly sophisticated.

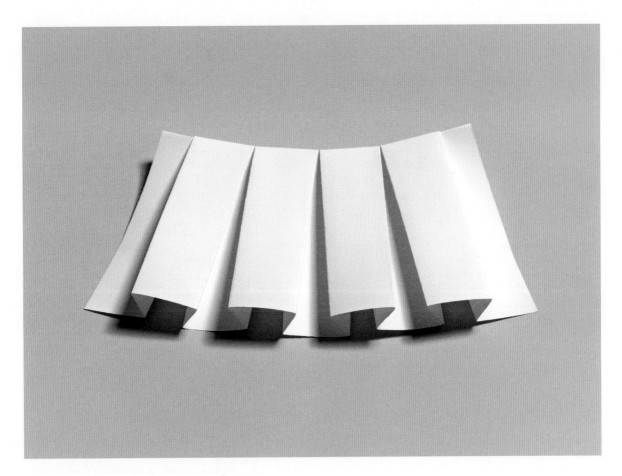

2.3.2_6
Like knife pleats (see 'Gathering and
Spreading', page 92), box pleats can also be
gathered flat along one edge and the other
be allowed to stretch open. All the knife pleat
examples in that section can be tried with
box pleats.

This piece in bronze is a collaboration between an origami designer and a sculptor specializing in metal casting. The design is first folded in paper, then cast in bronze, by a process that captures a high level of detail. It features a succession of box pleats that taper towards the bottom of the pot. Note the detail around the opening at the top. Diameter: 22cm (9in). Designed by Robert Lang (origami) and Kevin Box (bronze casting) (USA).

2.4
Upright Pleats

Upright pleats are the entry point to many advanced and open-ended pleat forms and surfaces. Their ability to stand vertically or to flatten to either side makes them unusually versatile, perhaps more so than any other pleat. Upright pleats are also the basis for the cut pleat, at the end of the chapter.

2.4.1   Basic Examples

2.4.1_1
The upright pleat has a three-fold 'valley-mountain-valley' cycle that enables the pleat to rise perpendicularly from the surface below. Note that the mountain fold is always midway between the two valleys.

2.4.1_2
This is the linear form of the upright pleat crease pattern.

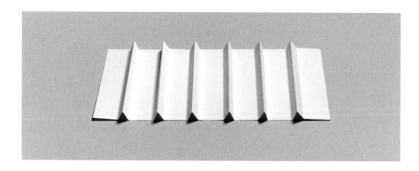

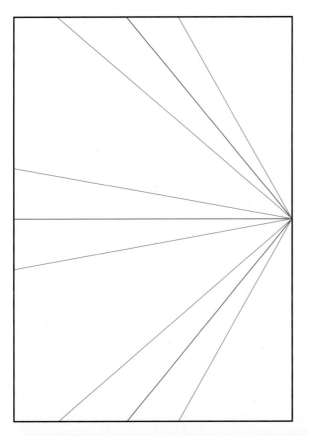

2.4.1_3
Upright pleats can also be made in rotational form. As before, any number of pleats can be made around any number of degrees of material.

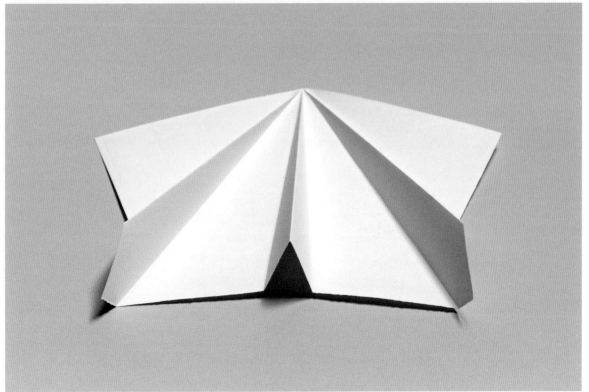

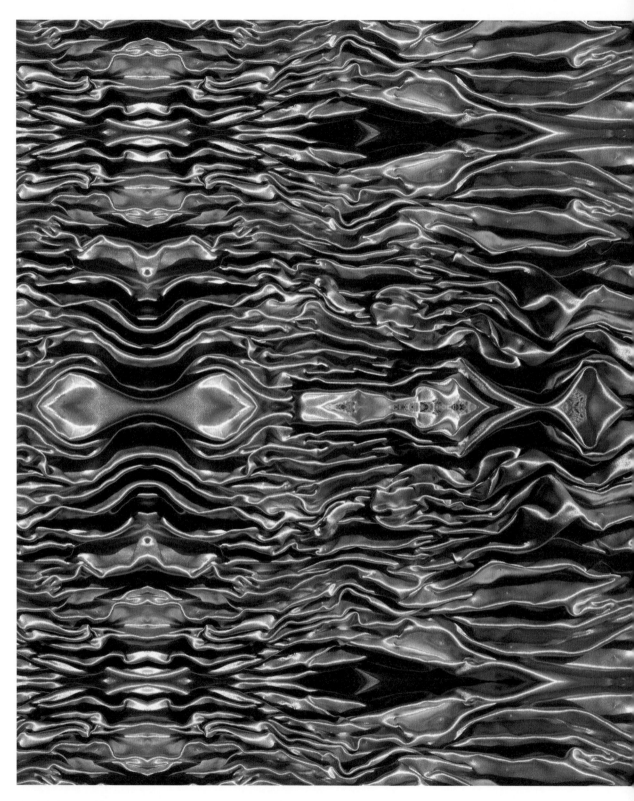

This digital print on fabric was assembled in Adobe PhotoShop from scans of semi-crumpled upright pleats made in a reflective fabric, creating a piece that is both extremely luxuriant, but also a little disturbing, especially when seen at its full size of 1m (39in) wide. Designed by Iris Haggai. Student project, Department of Textile Design, Shenkar College, Tel Aviv (Israel).

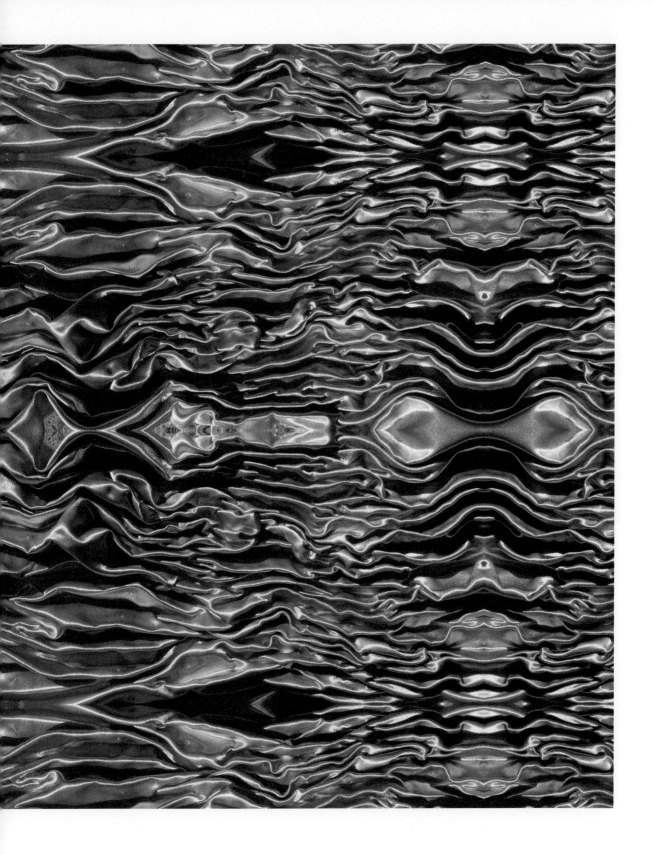

These two designs both use upright pleats to gather and release the fabric, and contrast precise, straight-line stitching with soft, billowing forms. Designed by Shani Levy (top) and Gily Seder (bottom). Student projects, Department of Fashion Design, Shenkar College, Tel Aviv (Israel).

2.4.2   Advanced Examples

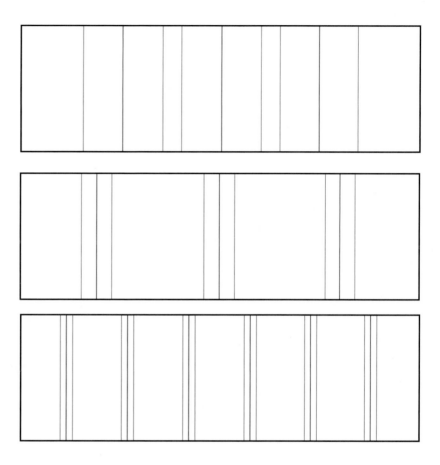

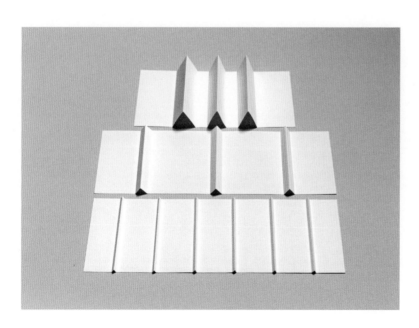

2.4.2_1
The three-fold cycle of an upright pleat
can be placed any distance part. Here are
three examples.

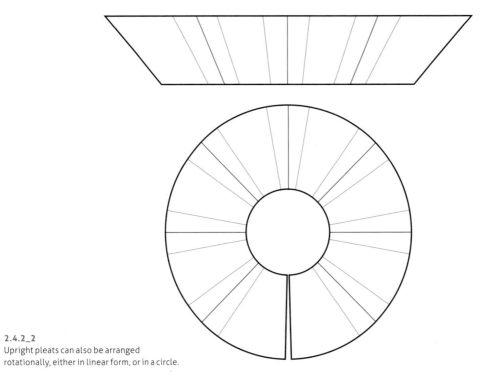

2.4.2_2
Upright pleats can also be arranged
rotationally, either in linear form, or in a circle.

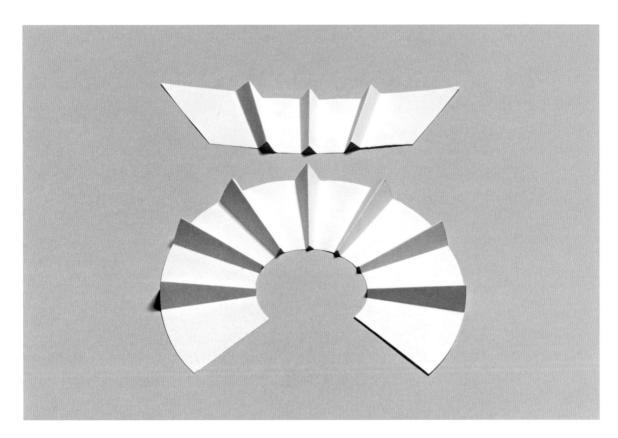

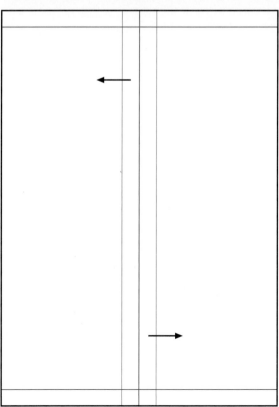

2.4.2_3
An interesting characteristic of the upright pleat is that it can be made to twist from side to side. For this simple example, make an upright pleat down the middle of the material. Twist the pleat flat to the left at the top, and to the right at the bottom. Trap the pleat flat by creating horizontal mountain folds near the top and bottom edges. The effect can look a little clumsy in paper, but works better in fabric.

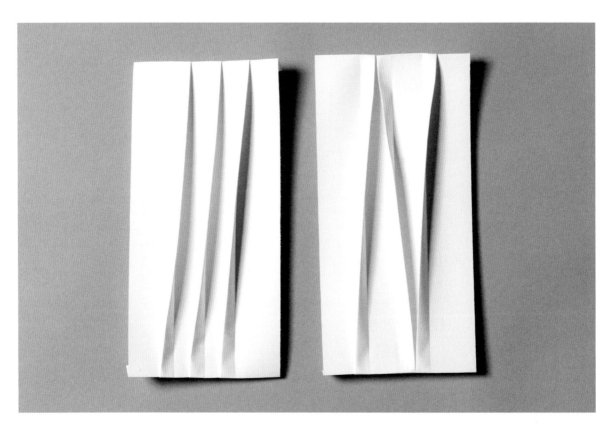

2.4.2_4
Developing the twisting idea introduced
in the previous example, different surface
patterns can be created, depending on
whether the pleats are twisted to the right
or to the left, in relation to their neighbours.

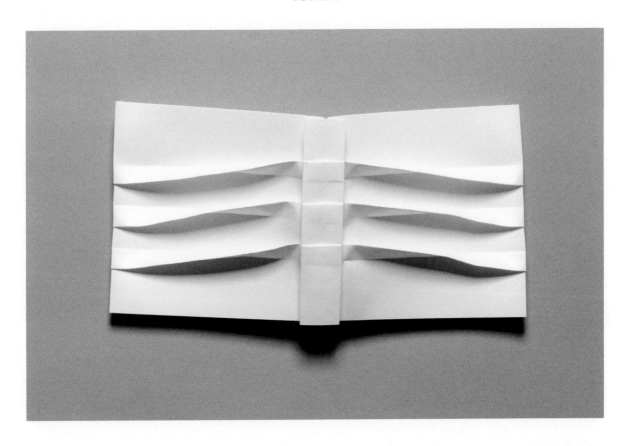

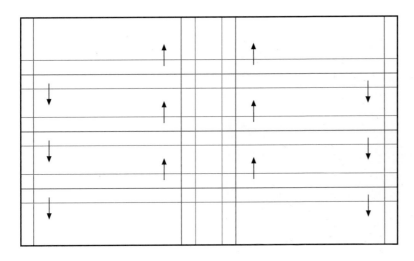

2.4.2_5
Before twisting the upright pleats, fold a box pleat across the middle of them. Unfold it. Twist only the upright pleats above the box pleat, as shown, then trap them flat by adding a horizontal mountain fold across the top edge, and by folding the box pleat. Repeat this with the bottom half of the paper. This way, the upright pleats are twisted first in one direction and then the other. The box pleat is a little clumsy, but it works well with paper. If using fabric, simply twist the pleats flat and then secure the top, middle and bottom positions of the pleats using three lines of stitches.

Above and left
The two images here show 100 per cent wool felt pleated and twisted back and forth, in subtly shifting patterns that appear to shimmer in the light. The designer has used the technique described on the previous spread to create a striking wall covering, which also dampens acoustics. Length: 4m (156in). Designed by Anne Kyrö Quinn (UK).

This cocktail dress features knife and
upright pleats that grow in width as they run
downwards from the shoulder, progressively
pulled and stretched out of shape. The dress,
from Alice Palmer's 'Fossil Warriors'
collection (UK), takes its inspiration
from ammonite fossils.

2.5
Non-parallel Linear Pleats

Non-parallel linear pleats take the stately parallel folds of accordion and knife pleats and twist them into interesting angles. The results can be dynamic and unique, but they can also sometimes look like unattractive doodles. The possibilities, though, are almost endless.

2.5.1   Basic Examples

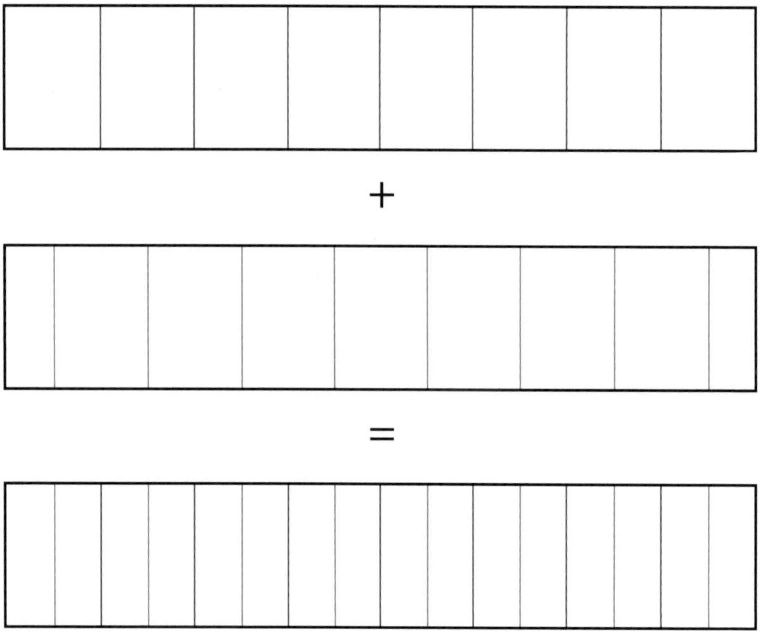

+

=

2.5.1_1
All the examples so far described in this book have featured mountain and valley folds in which every fold is parallel to every other fold. That is, all the mountain folds are parallel to each other, all the valley folds are parallel to each other, and the mountain and valley sets are parallel to each other. The pattern shown here describes a simple accordion pleat, but it also applies to box and upright pleats.

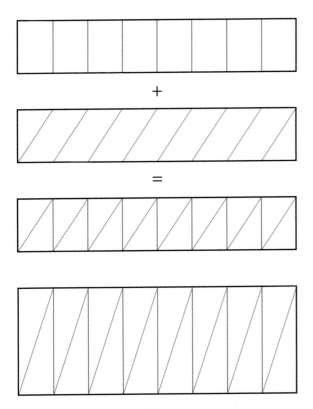

2.5.1_2
However, it is possible to change the principle of making every fold parallel to every other fold. In this example, the mountain folds remain vertical and parallel, while the valleys remain parallel but have become angled. The result is a zigzag pattern in which the mountain and valley folds connect. The pattern can be squashed or stretched. The result of this simple change is that innumerable new pleat patterns become possible.

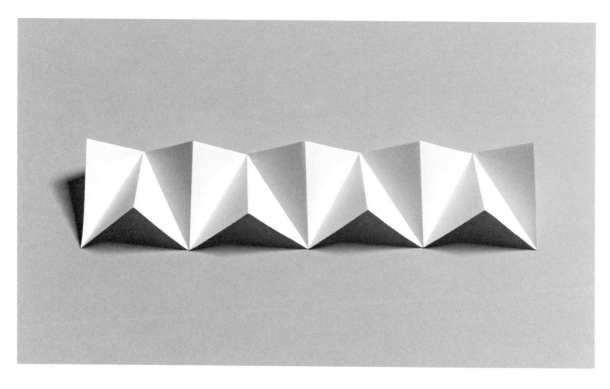

2.5.1_3
Exploring the non-parallel idea further, the line of angled valley folds that were all parallel to each other in the previous example have now been redesigned so that they create one unbroken zigzag line. Each alternate fold has been reflected vertically through 90 degrees.

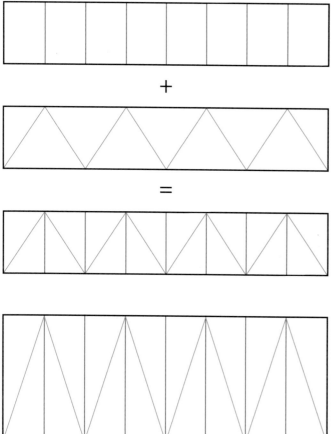

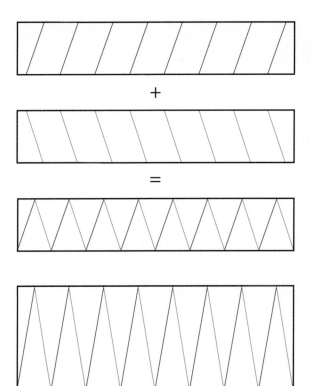

+

=

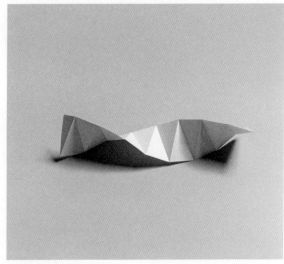

2.5.1_4
Just as the valleys can be angled, so can the
mountains. In this simple example, both the
mountains and the valleys have been rotated
by the same number of degrees away from
the vertical – the mountains clockwise and
the valleys anti-clockwise.

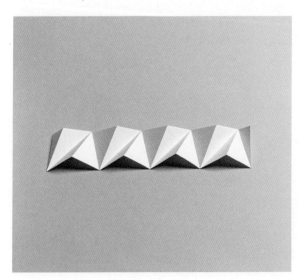

2.5.1_5
This example is similar to 2.5.1_3 opposite,
except now the mountains are slanting, not
vertical like before.

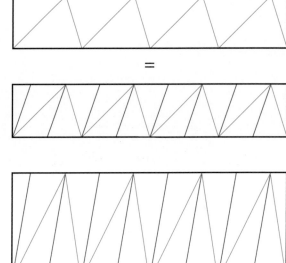

+

=

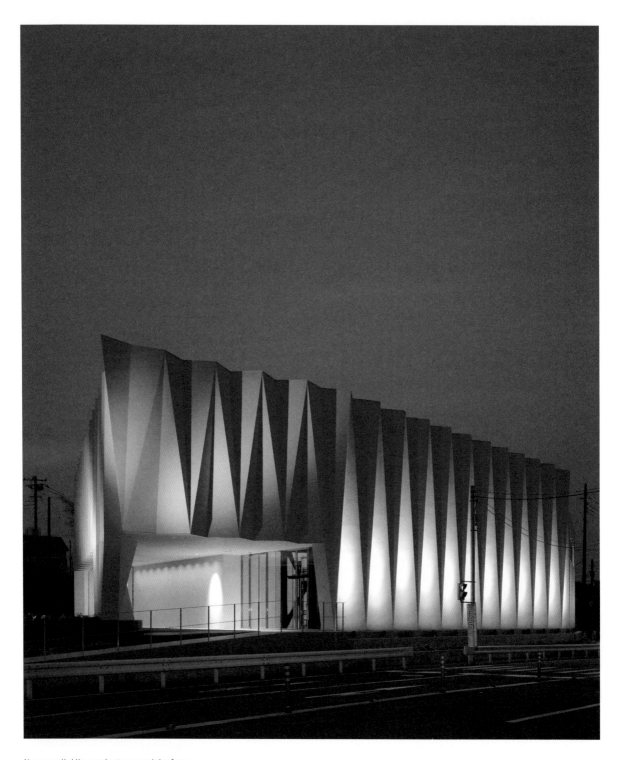

Non-parallel linear pleats around the four
sides of the building are used to dramatic
effect on the façade of this wedding centre.
The pleated theme is continued inside
the building (see opposite). Designed by
Hironaka Ogawa & Associates (Japan).

The pleated pattern first experienced on the exterior walls of the building (see opposite) is repeated internally at different scales and in different materials, on lighting (this page), and on dividing walls and ceilings. Designed by Hironaka Ogawa & Associates (Japan).

2.5.2 Advanced Examples

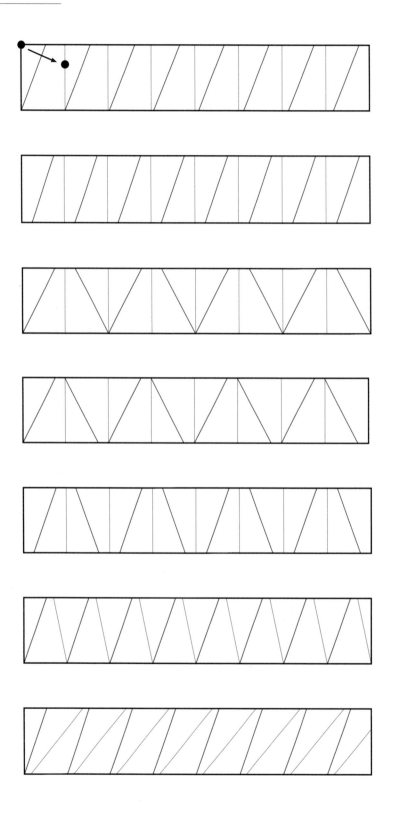

2.5.2_1
There are many possibilities for subtly different
zigzag patterns if the mountain and valley folds
do not meet at either the top or bottom edges,
or both. If you are looking for a creative
challenge, try to adapt some of these angled
patterns as knife, box or upright pleats.

Of the seven crease patterns illustrated on
the facing page, the first and fifth are shown
photographed above.

Opposite
This dramatic 11-m- (36-ft-) high stainless
steel sculpture in Paternoster Square,
central London, hides two air vents above
a subterranean electricity sub-station.
Whatever the weather and lighting
conditions, the sculpture always looks its
best. It uses the non-parallel linear pleats
described in this chapter to great effect and
was created from experiments with A4 paper.
Designed by Thomas Heatherwick (UK).

Above
Created as a prop for dancers to interact with,
this 5m (16ft) translucent spiral of fabric and
articulating bamboo canes would bend,
twist, wind up as a flat disk, stretch out and
billow as the performance progressed.
Designed by Jill Townsley for Risk Dance
Company (UK).

2.6
Curved Pleats

Curved pleats are a black art, a parallel universe in which surfaces heave and buckle in unpredictable ways, notoriously difficult to control and to understand. However, they are also fun, intuitive and beautiful, more akin to drawing (with a knife) than to folding. With a little practice, you will learn to position curved pleats so that they sit harmoniously together.

2.6.1   Basic Examples

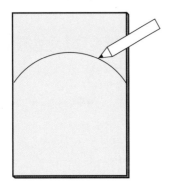

2.6.1_1
On a sheet of thick card, such as that from a cereal packet, use geometry equipment to draw an accurate curve.

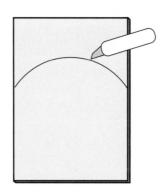

2.6.1_2
With extreme care, cut along the line of the curve as smoothly as possible.

2.6.1_3
This is the result. If the curve is rough when made by hand, try to make it using a mechanical method.

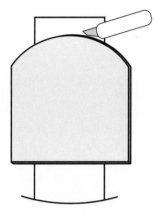

2.6.1_4
Place the card template on thin card.
To make the curved fold, use the back of a
scalpel or other narrow edge, as described
in 'How to Cut and Fold' (see page 17).
Carefully draw around the curve.

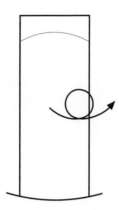

2.6.1_5
The curved crease – not yet folded into 3D
– will later be a valley fold, so to continue
the pleat, the next curved fold must be a
mountain. Therefore, to continue to make the
curved folds on the valley side only, the card
must be turned over, so that the next crease
is made on the other side of the card.

2.6.1_6
Note that on this side, the existing curved
crease is a mountain. Now make a second
curve. This will be a valley, relative to the
existing mountain.

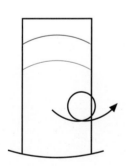

2.6.1_7
Turn over again.

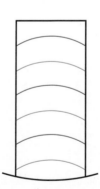

2.6.1_8
Continue the pattern, turning the card over
after each new curved crease is made to
make the next one.

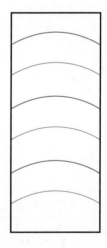

2.6.1_9
This is the completed pattern. The exact
number of curves you make is unimportant.

Subtle and elegant, this deceptively
simple-looking paper sculpture
demonstrates how complex forms can be
made from a simple folded pattern, in this
case, a series of concentric curved pleats.
Designed by Matt Shlian (USA).

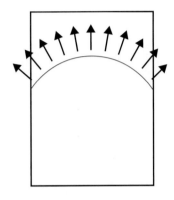

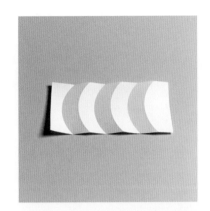

2.6.1_10
To make a curved fold, hold the card with the mountain side uppermost. Slowly squeeze the curve, pinch by pinch, from one end to the other, bending back the card that lies outside the curve. This can take a little practice. The result will be a convex curve above the fold and a concave fold beneath it.

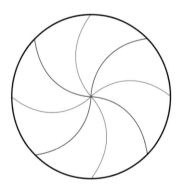

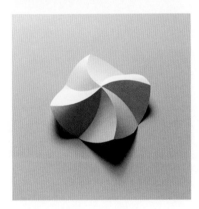

2.6.1_11
Curved pleats can also be made rotationally. It can take practice and some skill to pack them close together, so for your early attempts limit your patterns to the eight shown here.

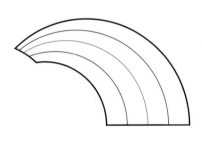

2.6.1_12
An interesting effect is achieved by tapering the curved pleat. Each arc has its own radius, so a pattern such as this should be drawn with a pair of compasses, and each crease cut separately from thick card.

2.6.2   Advanced Examples

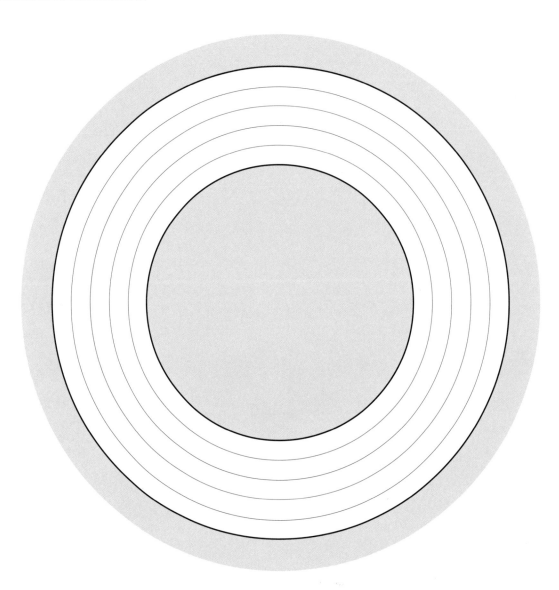

2.6.2_1
A particularly fascinating curved example is
this circle, which has had its centre removed.
A series of complete folded circles will distort
the 2D plane into a 3D form. The simplest
form is a saddle, but if the hole is enlarged
and the number of circular folds increased,
the surface will distort even more into
a figure-of-eight, and even into several
complete loops, like those seen on an extreme
roller coaster ride. These forms are best made
using a plotter or laser cutter, both to save
labour and to guarantee absolute accuracy.

2.6.2_2
The placement of curved waves in a parallel arrangement creates a particularly attractive surface when carefully lit. It is a curved relative of a full V-pleat grid (see Chapters 4 and 5).

Like the V-pleat grid, it can – perhaps surprisingly – be concertinaed together until almost flat. The surface is remarkably dynamic and expressive.

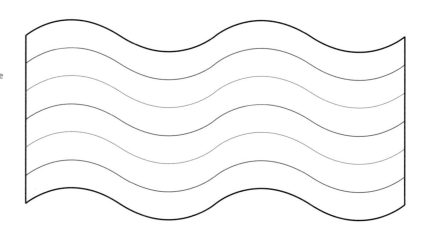

Several examples of the distorted ring
described on the previous spread were
interlocked to create this carefully composed
mass of writhing, swirling curves entitled
'Sprouting'. Note how the rings are different
sizes and have different numbers of curved
creases. Dimensions: height 25cm (14in).
Designed by Erik and Marty Demaine (USA).

2.7

Cut Pleats

Cut pleats can initially seem to be the undisciplined younger sibling of the pleats family – a little innocent and rather wild. However, when used in combination, they suddenly mature to become sophisticated and complex. The introduction of a cut into the folding pattern creates many exciting new opportunities for surfaces.

2.7.1   Basic Examples

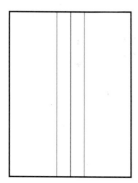

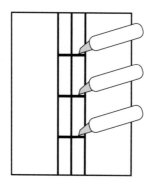

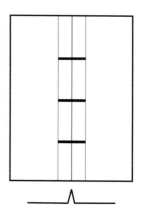

2.7.1_1
Create a simple upright pleat (see page 110).

2.7.1_2
Make three cuts between the valley folds. The number and exact placement of the cuts is unimportant.

2.7.1_3
Ignore the three cuts and make the upright pleat.

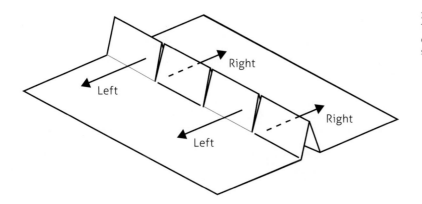

2.7.1_4
This is how the paper looks. The three cuts divide the pleat into four sections. Flatten the sections alternately left, right, left, right …

2.7.1_5
… like this. The paper is now flat again. If the pleats do not lie very flat, turn the paper over and rub the back surface. This will reinforce the folds.

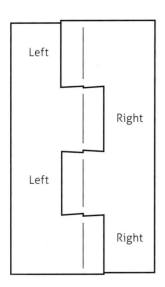

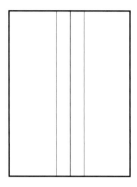

2.7.1_6
An alternative way to make the cuts is as
follows. Make the upright pleat, as before.

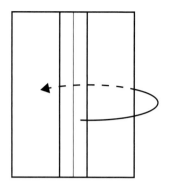

2.7.1_7
Make only the mountain fold, folding the
paper in half.

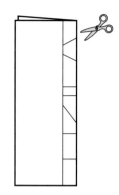

2.7.1_8
Using scissors (or a knife), make a series of
cuts from the mountain fold to the valley
folds. The cuts can be horizontal, at an angle,
curved ... anything you want.

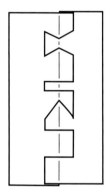

2.7.1_9
Refold the upright pleat to look like Step 4,
then flatten the pleats left, right, left, right ...,
as before. The pattern is surprisingly complex.

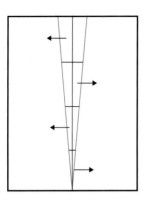

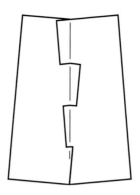

2.7.1_10
Cut pleats can also be made radially.

2.7.1_11
For a more dramatic effect, increase the
angle of the V in Step 10.

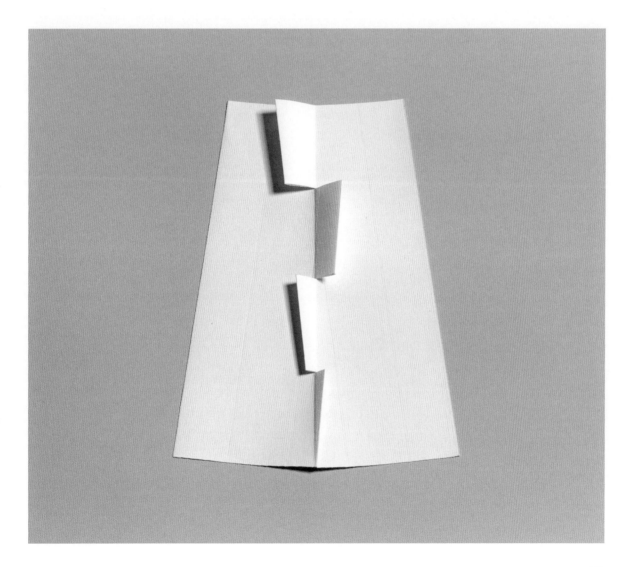

2.7.2   Advanced Examples

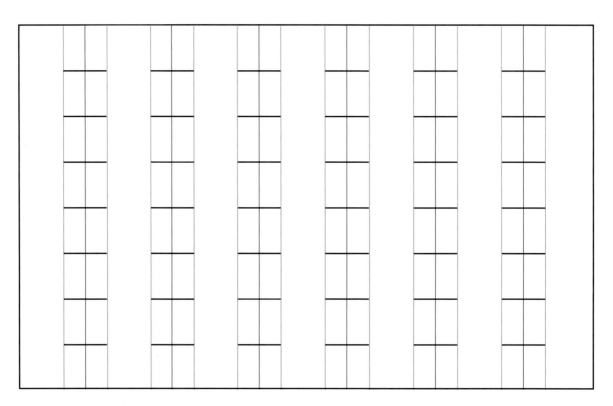

2.7.2_1
Complex surfaces can be built up by making
a series of parallel upright pleats, which
are developed into cut pleats. The grid cut
pattern seen here can create two different
surfaces, depending on how the 'left, right'
patterns fall on neighbouring pleats.

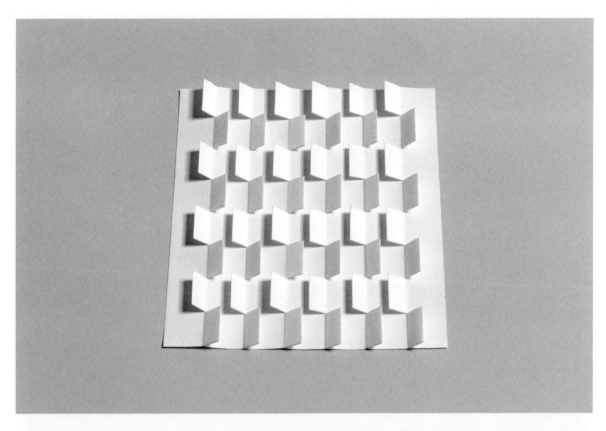

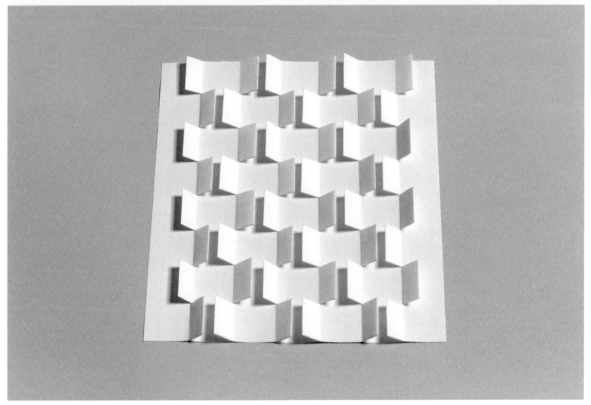

2.7.3 Cut Pleats as Pop-ups

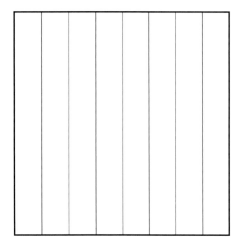

2.7.3_1
Divide a square (or rectangle) of paper
into an accordion pleat, divided into eighths.
The mountain folds are at the left and
right edges.

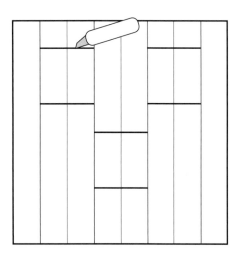

2.7.3_2
Make three pairs of cuts, as shown. Note how
the cuts are on the 'back' of an upright pleat,
whereas previously, they were on the 'front'.

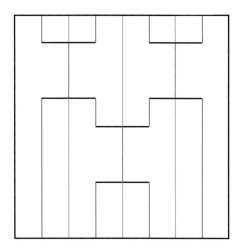

2.7.3_3
Make all the pleats as shown, but removing
six short sections of crease. Note the three,
new, short mountain folds between the three
pairs of cuts. Then, when everything is folded
simultaneously, a cut pop-up form will emerge.

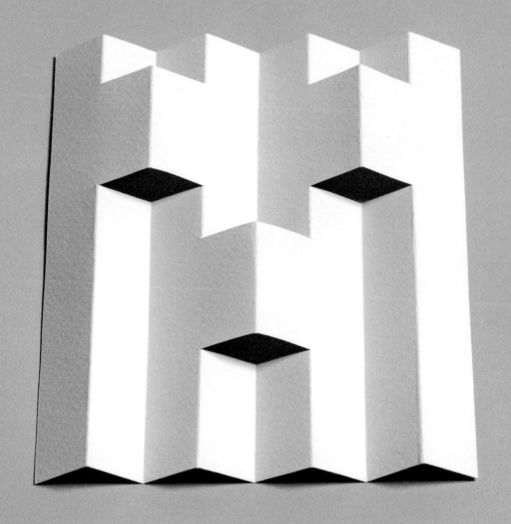

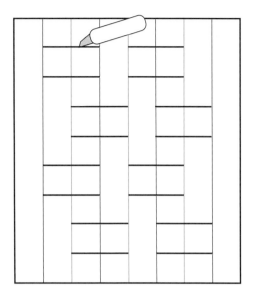

2.7.3_4
Whereas the two pop-up forms on the top row of the previous example were three folds apart, the cuts in this new example are only one fold apart. The effect is to create both positive and negative pop-ups. Create the pattern carefully.

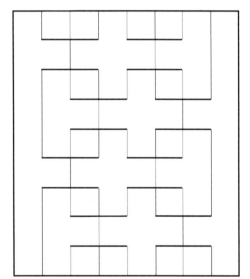

2.7.3_5
As before, make all the pleats as shown, noting that 16 short sections will not be folded, and that between the two cuts in each pair, the fold is reversed.

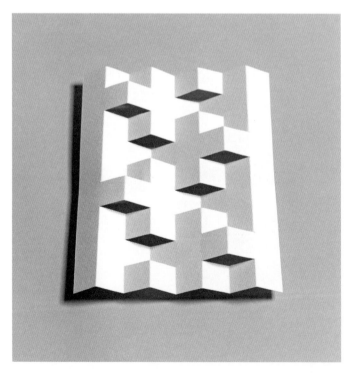

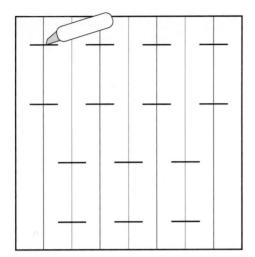

2.7.3_6
A further example is to create a simple accordion pleat, but without fully extending the cuts in the manner of an upright pleat. In this example, pairs of cuts terminate midway between the vertical folds.

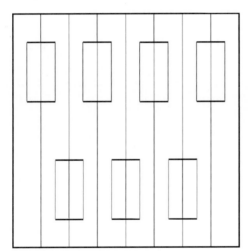

2.7.3_7
Now create new folds that connect the ends of the cuts within each pair. This divides the paper into 16 across its width. Note how some new folds are mountains and some are valleys.

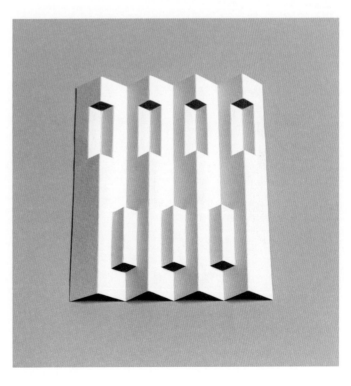

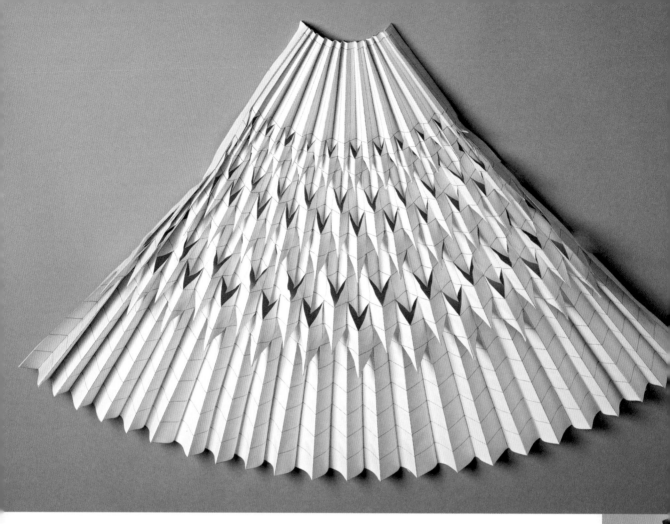

Above
A paper template – one of two identical templates – from which the fabric skirt on the facing page was made. In both sheets, radial accordion pleats were cut open in a repeat pattern. Using the steaming technique described in Chapter 7, the fabric was first pleated and then cut to shape to create the final design. Designed by Liat Greenberg. Student project, Department of Fashion Design, Shenkar College, Tel Aviv (Israel).

Below
The strict geometric patterns created in the
paper template on the facing page become
much more informal when made in fabric.
As the wearer moves, ever-changing points
of light become visible through the skirt,
creating an unexpected sparkling effect.

3

TWISTED PLEATS

Twisted Pleats

The subject of twisted pleats could be a continuation of the 'Basics Pleats' chapter, but since there are so many ways to twist a pleat, it really deserves a chapter of its own.

For the first time in this book it may be necessary to measure angles with a pencil, ruler and protractor. You may even prefer to draw them with CAD software in a computer, print out the drawing, then cut it out and fold it up. Nevertheless, wherever possible, you are advised to continue to work by hand – it is quicker and more fluent than using geometry equipment or a digital aid. Some of the constructions, particularly towards the end of the chapter, become geometrically sophisticated, but with patience and study, the secrets of their structures will become apparent.

This chapter explores how simple 2D rosettes can be stacked, how they can transform into 3D columns and how these columns can finally evolve into stunning ring columns. Each section in the chapter builds on what has gone before, so for a full understanding of twisted pleats, you are advised – as always – to work through sequentially from the first page to the last.

This is the one genre of pleating that has yet to be explored in any depth by designers. For that reason, this chapter contains few examples of finished design work. If you are looking for an area to specialize in, twisted pleats may be for you.

3.1
Twisted Rosettes

Of the many ways to twist pleats explored in this chapter, twisted rosettes are the simplest example. Even if you wish to make something from later in the chapter, it is highly recommended that you first make something from this section to understand the basic principles of how twisted pleats are constructed and twisted.

3.1_1
A twisted rosette is a tube of material which is designed to twist *flat*. The pattern of valley-mountain folds is fundamentally the same as described in 'Non-parallel Linear Pleats' (see page 126). The key part of the design is the angle of the valley fold, relative to the number of sides of the tube.

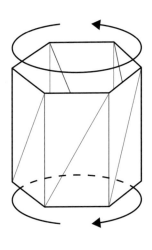

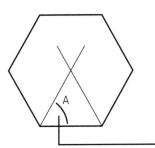

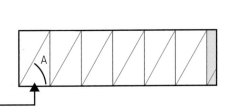

3.1_2
In the example above, the tube has six sides. If we draw a hexagon to represent the tube, the angle from a corner to the centre point of the hexagon is angle A, which is 60 degrees (for a hexagon only). Thus, when making the six-sided tube, angle A (the angle of the valley fold to the horizontal) will be 60 degrees. Note that the material has a small piece added to the right-hand edge to enable the tube to be glued shut.

155

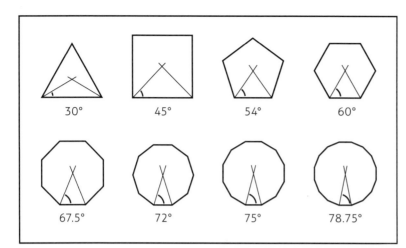

3.1_3
Depending on the number of sides of the tube, the angle of the valley folds to the horizontal will change and, thus, the proportion of the tube will change. The greater the number of sides, the greater the angle.

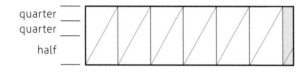

3.1_4
An interesting variation is to make a tube and to measure the half and top quarter.

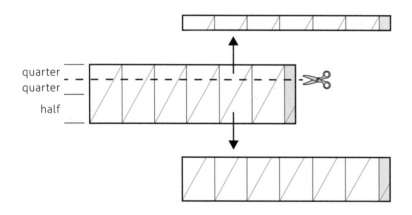

3.1_5
Cut off the top quarter, separating the tube into two unequal pieces. When twisted into flat rosettes, the three-quarters section will create a secondary rosette around the centre point (which exposes the back face of the material) and the one-quarter will create a hexagonal ring.

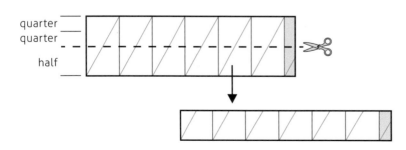

3.1_6
Trimming the tube into equal halves will create two identical pieces. However, the lack of an overlap around the centre point will not lock the rosette flat. Without something to hold the flaps in place, it will open.

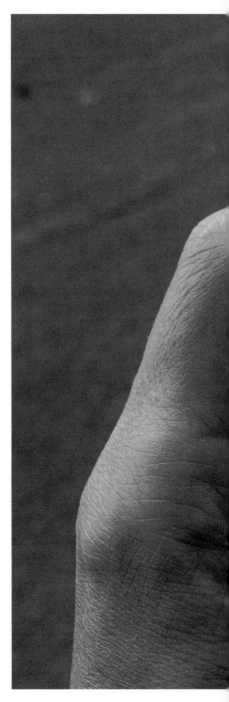

Above
One of a series of designs that can collapse
flat for storage and untwist into a 3D form
for use, these mathematically pleated light
shades offer a harmonious balance between
light and shade, strength and grace, and
geometry and natural form. The 'open'
form of the same design is shown on pages
152–53. Dimensions: diameter, 44cm
(17.5in), length when open, 50cm (20in).
Designed by Issey Miyake (Japan) for
Artemide (Italy).

Above
This beautiful twisted pleat follows the
geometric principles described in this
chapter, with the addition of vertical
sides. These transform a 2D twist into
a 3D box-like form. The twist repeats on
the reverse. Note that there are 32 pleats;
readers who have read Chapter 1 will
recognize this number as significant.
Designed by Philip Chapman-Bell (USA).

3.2
Twisted Columns

Twisted columns are more intuitive to construct than the twisted rosettes of the previous section. They are also extremely rigid and strong. Some practice is required to twist them into shape. A tip is to make your first columns with just a few sides and to increase the number as you become more experienced.

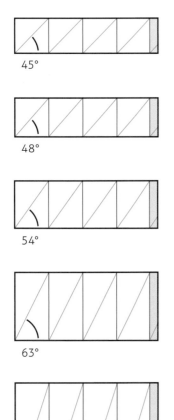

45°

48°

54°

63°

72°

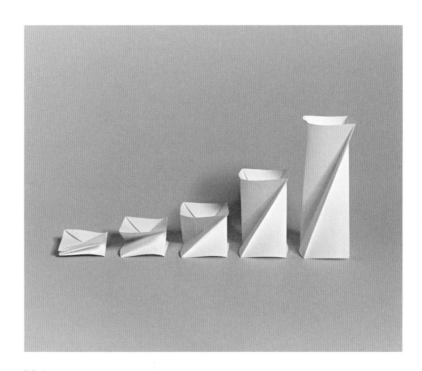

3.2_1

The twisted rosettes described previously lie flat because of the careful use of angled valley folds. Twisted columns use the same principle of a vertical mountain fold and an angled valley fold, but the angle of the valley is calculated to lift the rosette into 3D, as a column.

Shown here is a square tube. The top drawing shows the angle of the valley at 45 degrees. As described in 3.1_3, this specific angle on a four-sided tube will create a flat rosette.

If the angle is increased to 48 degrees, the rosette will no longer lie flat, but will rise a little into 3D. By increasing the angle further – the examples here show 54, 63 and 72 degrees, although they are somewhat arbitrary – the column will stand increasingly upright. In this way, its height can be carefully controlled.

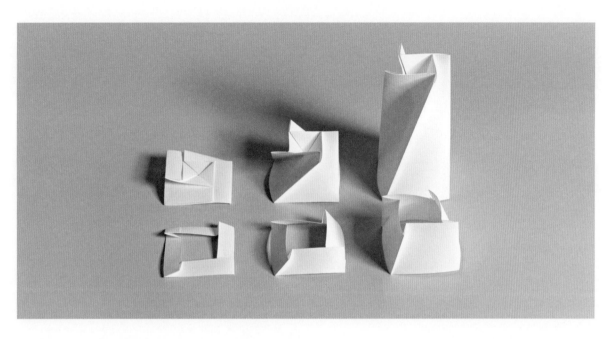

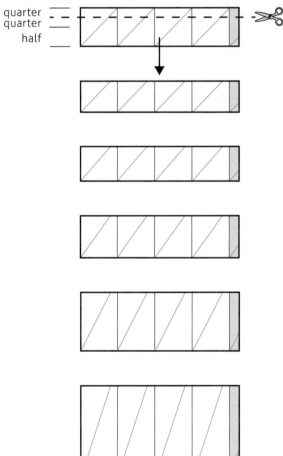

3.2_2
If one-quarter is cut off the full tube (see 3.1_4 and 3.1_5 in the preceding section), the column will have a more complex top. In the photograph, the removed top quarters have been placed in front of the columns made from the remaining three-quarters. Although discarded, the cut-off quarters are themselves of interest.

3.2_3

In this variation, the tube has eight sides.
A flat octagonal rosette – according to 3.1_3
– will have an angle of 67.5 degrees, so any
angle greater than this will lift the rosette into
a 3D column. The angle here is 70 degrees.
The additional 2.5 degrees may not seem
significant, but it is sufficient to raise the
rosette into a substantial column-type form.

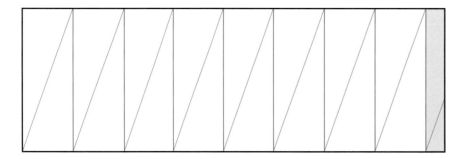

3.2_4
Columns (and rosettes) can be made not only
from linear pleats, but also from rotational
ones. In this example, the valley folds lie at
67.5 degrees to the bottom edge and the
mountain folds lie at 75 degrees.

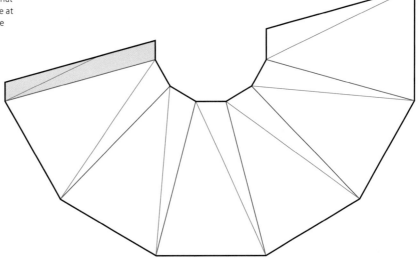

3.3

Stacked Rosettes and Columns

Stacked rosettes and columns are the natural progression from making the single examples in the two previous sections. Even when stacked, the structures continue to be strong.

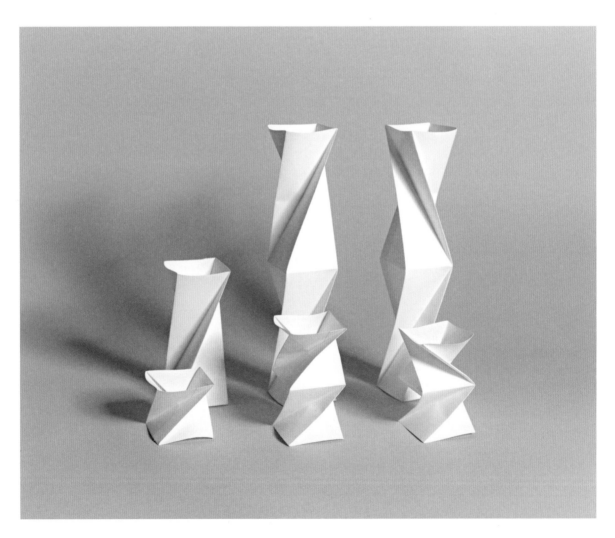

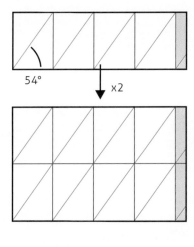

54°

x2

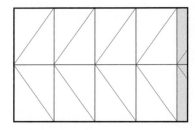

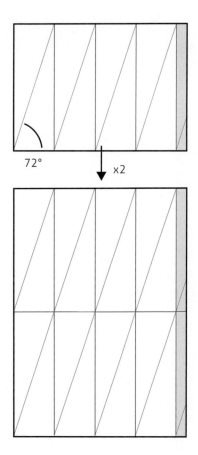

72°

x2

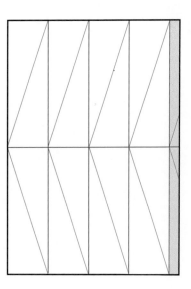

3.3_1
Whatever the angle of the valley fold to the
horizontal, and whatever the number of
sides the tube may have, when rosettes and
columns are made with a linear procession
of pleats, the top edge will always remain
parallel to the bottom edge. This means that
it is simple to stack rosettes and columns on
top of one another.

In the example shown here, a twisted square
column is made from valley fold angles of
54 and 72 degrees. The photo shows single
twisted columns on the left (the 54-degree
twist is at the front and the 72-degree twist
is at the back), as well as stacked examples in
the centre and on the right. Note how in the
examples back centre and front centre, the
stacked columns are identical in both layers,
whereas in the examples on the back right
and front right, the upper and lower twists in
each stack are mirror images of each other. It
is also possible to stack one angle of twist on
top of another angle, or to change the angle
each time. The stacking could be repeated
innumerable times.

Note: remember that, depending on the
material and the number of sides, it can
sometimes be very difficult to make the
rosettes twist flat.

3.4
Twisted Rings

Twisted rings are the entry point for making 3D twisted vessels. The principles of how they are constructed can seem a little esoteric, but when understood, many beautiful and fascinating pleated forms can be made.

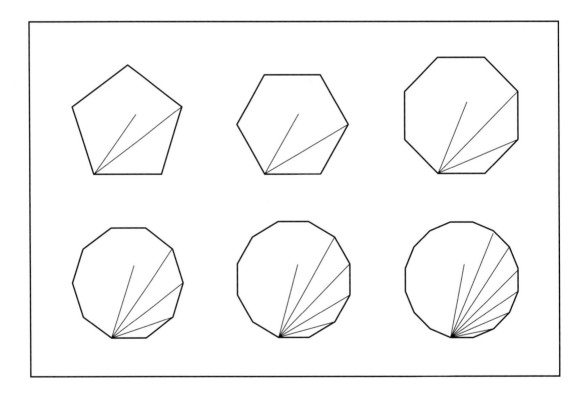

3.4_1
Each polygon has a unique number of diagonals radiating from each corner, one of which goes through the centre point (for an odd-sided polygon such as a pentagon, the centre point is not on a diagonal line, but the line is still relevant when making twisted rings). Only the diagonal through the centre and the diagonals with lesser angles are relevant – the diagonal lines on the other side of the centre line are not. A twisted ring will use two of these diagonal lines.

3.4_2

In this example, we are using the only two diagonals available with a hexagon. Angle A is 60 degrees and angle B is 30 degrees. Every example will have two different angles called A and B.

A strip is constructed in six parts (because the polygon is a hexagon), and the mountain and valley folds are constructed at angles of 60 and 30 degrees to the vertical. This will created a hexagonal twisted ring.

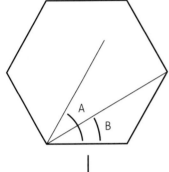

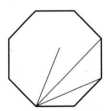

3.4_3

With eight sides and three possible diagonals, an octagon offers more possibilities to make a twisted ring than the hexagon above. Here are the three angles of the three diagonals.

67.5°

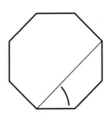

45°

22.5°

3.4_4
Like the hexagonal example in 3.4_2, we need to create two angles – angle A and angle B. The three possible choices for A + B are:
67.5° + 45°
45° + 22.5°
67.5° + 22.5°
The first two examples create octagonal rings. However, oddly, the final example makes a square (four-sided) ring. The reason is based on the difference between the angles of 67.5 and 22.5 degrees being 45 degrees, which is the angle from the corner of a square to the centre point. Thus, only four sections are needed, not eight.

67.5° + 45°

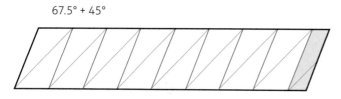

45° + 22.5°

67.5° + 22.5°

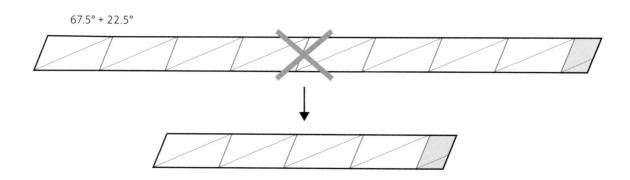

75°   60°   45°   30°   15°

3.4_5
As the number of sides increases, so does the number of diagonals and hence the number of possible combinations for A + B. Here, a dodecagon (a 12-sided polygon) has five diagonals and thus a possible ten combinations of A + B.

75° + 60°

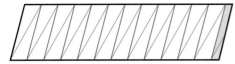

60° + 45°

45° + 30°

30° + 15°

3.4_6
In 3.4_3 and 3.4_4 we saw how the third example created a difference between the angles of 45 degrees, so the ring was only four-sided, not eight-sided.

In the four examples shown here, the difference between A and B is 15 degrees. Subtracting 15 degrees from 90 degrees creates an angle of 75 degrees, which is the angle between the corner of a *dodecagon* and the line to the centre point. So, since this angle is 75 degrees, there must be 12 sections to each strip and each edge of the dodecagon is described by a section of the strip.

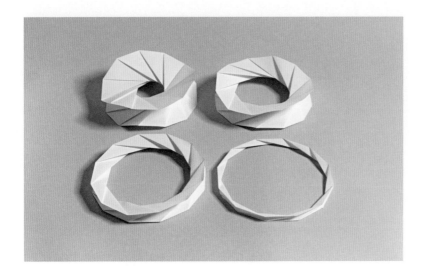

75° + 45°

60° + 30°

45° + 15°

3.4_7
In these three examples, the difference between A and B is now 30 degrees. Subtracting 30 degrees from 90 degrees creates an angle of 60 degrees, which is the angle between the corner of a *hexagon* and the line to the centre point. So, since this angle is 60 degrees, there must be only six sections that describe the dodecagon (describing every second edge) and thus only six sections to the strip.

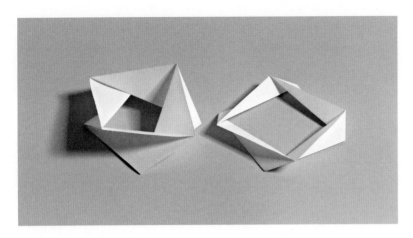

3.4_8
In these two examples, the difference between A and B is now 45 degrees. Subtracting 45 degrees from 90 degrees creates an angle of 45 degrees, which is the angle between the corner of a *square* and the line to the centre point. So, since this angle is 45 degrees, there must be only four sections that describe the dodecagon (that describe every third edge) and thus only four sections to the strip.

75° + 30°

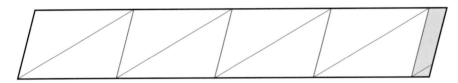

60° + 15°

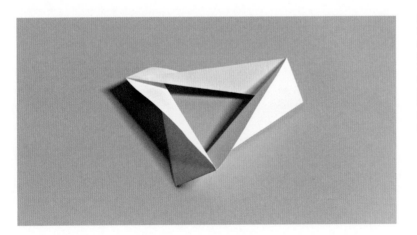

3.4_9
In this one example, the difference between A and B is now 60 degrees. Subtracting 60 degrees from 90 degrees creates an angle of 30 degrees, which is the angle between the corner of a *triangle* and the line to the centre point. So, since this angle is 60 degrees, there must be only 3 sections that describe the dodecagon (that describe every fourth edge) and thus only 3 sections to the strip.

75° + 15°

3.5

Stacked Rings

Stacked rings are simply the stacking of the twisted rings made in the previous section.

3.5_1
Here, an octagonal twisted ring is stacked ring on ring, eight times. The A and B angles are 67.5 and 45 degrees. The whole structure can be compressed flat, although under natural tension it will want to expand into 3D.

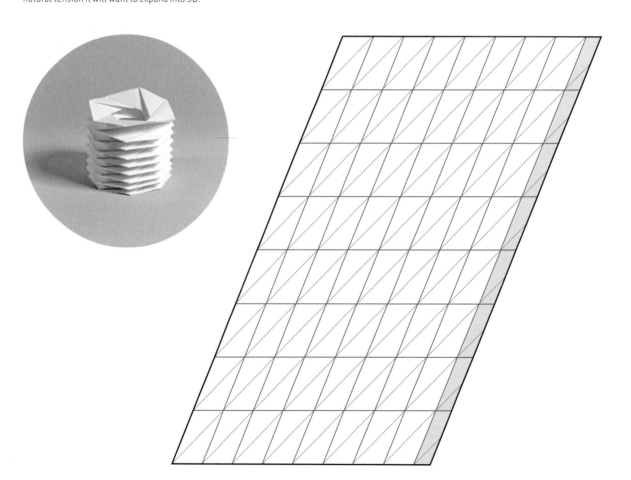

3.5_2
In this second example, a square twisted ring with A and B angles of 67.5 and 22.5 degrees has eight repeats stacked one on another.

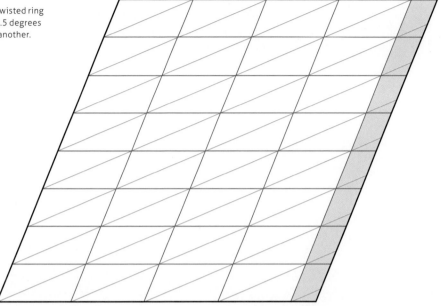

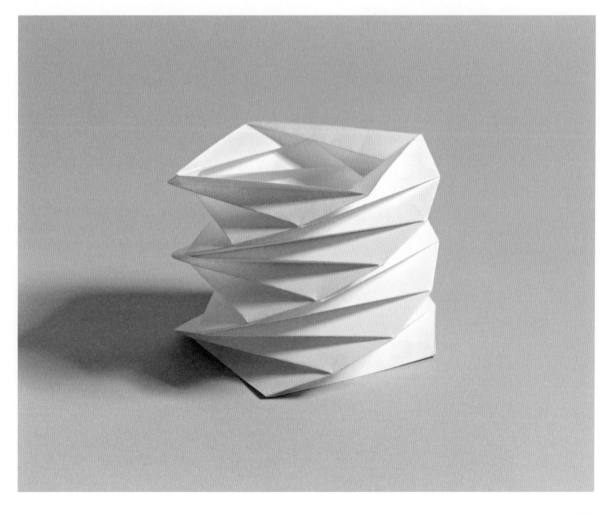

A grid of equilateral triangles create a
configuration of stacked rings (see previous
spread). Made in strong paper and 75cm
(30in) high, this floor-standing light makes
an attractive object even when not lit
from within. Designed by Lampshado
(Czech Republic).

3.6

Ring Columns

Ring columns are the technical culmination of this chapter. They are relatively intuitive to make, meaning that unlike twisted rings and stacked rings, they do not rely on exact angles for effect. Despite looking decorative and sometimes fragile, they are surprisingly rigid and strong.

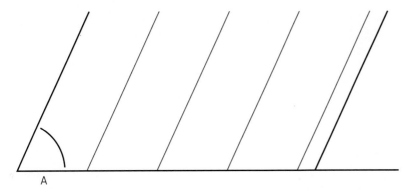

3.6_1
Ring columns are constructed from three different angles, A, B and C. This is angle A, the more upright of two sloping angles.

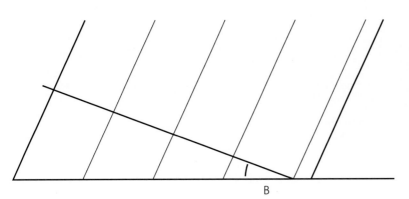

3.6_2
Angle B is less upright than angle A and crosses A on multiple occasions. Notice how in this configuration, A and B are on opposite sides of an imaginary vertical line – that is, A lines travel upwards and to the right, whereas the B line goes upwards and to the left.

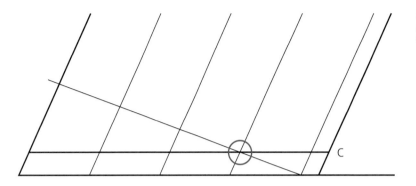

3.6_3
Angle C is horizontal and passes through where A and B intersect.

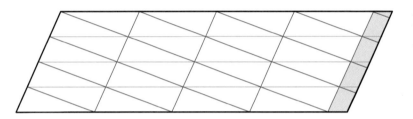

3.6_4
A full crease pattern can now be constructed. Notice how the A and B creases are mountain folds and C creases are valleys. The exact angles are unimportant.

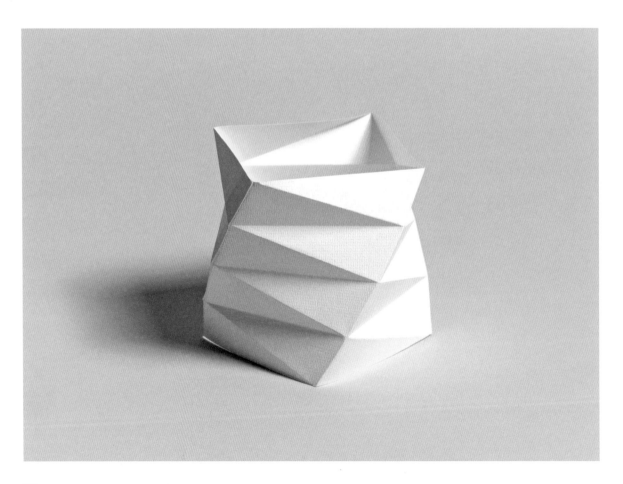

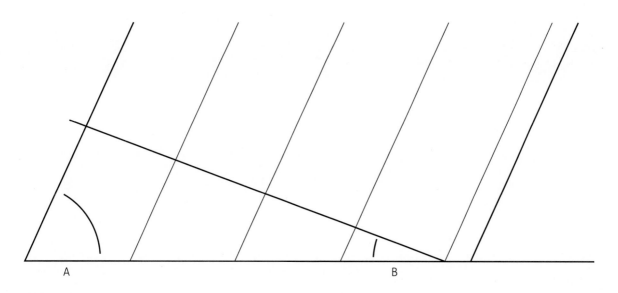

3.6_5
The A and B angles can differ greatly to
create a whole series of different columns.
The C lines are always horizontal.

3.6_6
Here, 3.6_4 is reproduced as the top drawing
of the three. When the B lines are removed,
the skeleton of the structure is exposed as a
series of parallelograms, as shown in the
second drawing. The B lines can now be
reintroduced, but this time across the other
diagonal of each parallelogram, as can be
seen in the third drawing.

Thus, whereas the diagonals in the first
drawings pass through the obtuse corners of
each parallelogram ('obtuse' means greater
than 90 degrees), in the third drawing they
pass through the acute corners ('acute'
means less than 90 degrees). Note, too, how
the distribution of mountains and valleys
differs between the two examples.

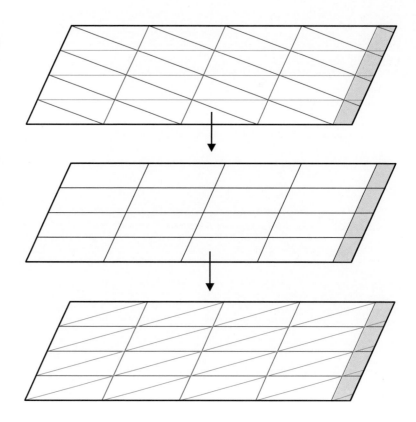

V–Pleats

Depending on your point of view, V-pleats are either the playground of pleating, or the assault course. For some they are fun and playful, whereas for others they can be fearsome and exhausting. It is an area of pleating where everyone finds their own level of technical involvement, be it simple, intermediate or advanced. Whatever the level, though, there is beauty to be found.

This chapter first explains the structure of the 'node' at the centre of a V-pleat. It should be understood fully if you wish to progress through the chapter, which goes on to describe how V-pleats can be used in combination, eventually building to a full grid.

The principles learnt here will enable you to create forms and surfaces that collapse flat and open out in a spectacular manner. V-pleats are inherently dynamic, but more than that, they are also beautiful and logical structures that delight the eye. They are the perfect combination of form, surface and function.

4.1

The Basic V

The basic V-pleat is the most common way to develop a simple line of pleats into surfaces and forms that are potentially very complex. The heart of the V-pleat is the node, where four separate folds meet. Made correctly, this node will collapse the sheet flat. Ultimately, as the chapter will show, this collapsing when repeated many times, will collapse flat very elaborate surfaces and forms.

4.1.1 Basic Construction

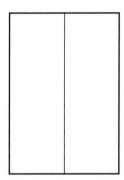

4.1.1_1
Create a 'universal fold' down the centre line (a universal fold is described on page 19).

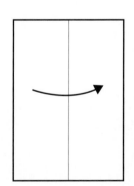

4.1.1_2
Fold in half.

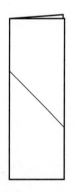

4.1.1_3
Now create a 45-degree universal fold.

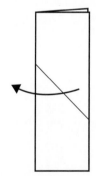

4.1.1_4
Unfold the paper.

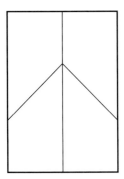

4.1.1_5
This is the crease pattern. Note that the V is upside down and all folds are universal folds.

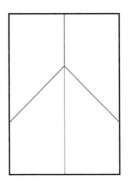

4.1.1_6
Individually refold the creases so that three folds are mountains and one is a valley. Note that the mountains create an inverted letter Y.

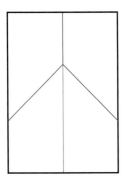 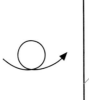 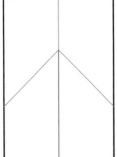

4.1.1_7
The pattern of three mountains and one valley is central to the structure of a V-pleat. When the sheet is turned over, the crease pattern is the opposite: now there are three valleys and one mountain. A V-pleat must always be one or the other.

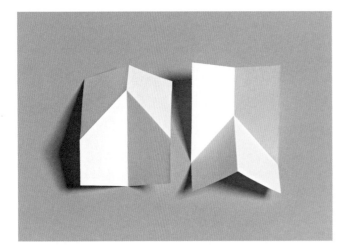

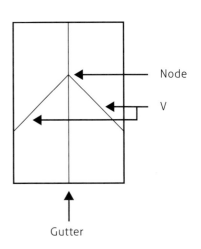

4.1.1_8
These are the three parts of a V-pleat:

Node: Where the four separate creases meet.

V: The sloping folds that meet at the node.

Gutter: The central line which changes from valley to mountain or mountain to valley when it crosses the node.

4.1.2   Changing the Angle of the V

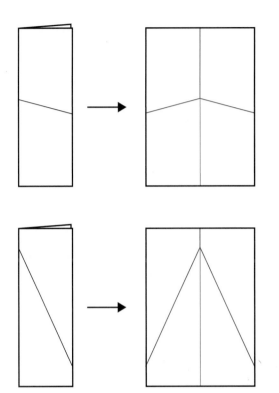

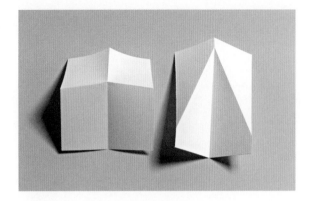

4.1.2_1
The angle of the V made in Step 3, on page
181, was at 45 degrees. However, the V-crease
can be made at almost any angle. In the first
example here, the angle of the V is large and in
the second, it is small. Note that to make either
example, you first make universal folds, as
described in the previous section.

4.1.3   Changing the Position of the Gutter

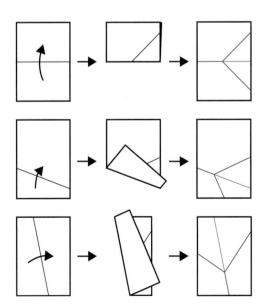

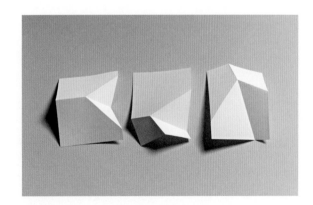

4.1.3_1
In both the sections above, the gutter ran
down the centre of the sheet. However, it can
be placed in any position at all, whether
symmetrical or asymmetrical. Here are three
examples, in which gutter folds are first made
and then crossed by a V.

4.1.4   Vs and Gutters in Combination

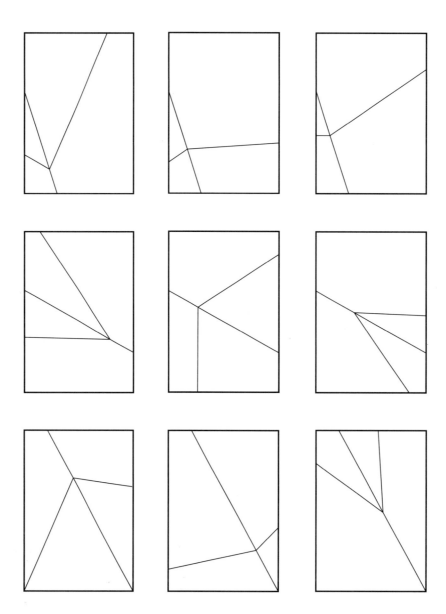

4.1.4_1
Each of these nine examples is made in two
stages: first a gutter fold is made, then a
V-fold is created through it. Each line of three
examples shows the gutter in the same place,
with the V in a different place. In this way, the
combination of gutter and V offer many
creative possibilities.

4.2

Multiple Gutters

Multiple gutters take the simple V-pleat described above and repeat it in a horizontal row. This is the first step in learning how to repeat the V as a grid.

4.2.1   Concept

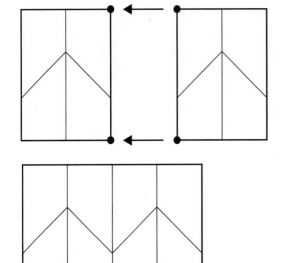

4.2.1_1
Two basic examples from the beginning of the chapter can be placed so that they touch.

4.2.1_2
The edge where they joined now becomes part of the total crease pattern. Note how the two upturned Vs have joined to create a letter M.

4.2.1_3
More individual Vs can be joined together to create a horizontal line with an infinite number of repeats.

4.2.2   Basic Construction

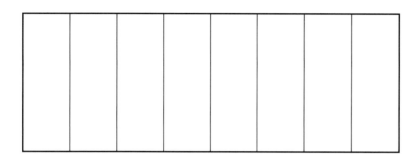

4.2.2_1
Create eight accordion pleats. Make them all universal folds.

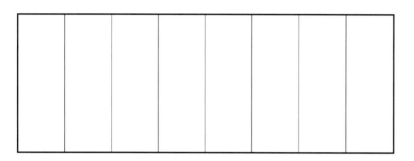

4.2.2_2
Refold the universal folds as a regular accordion pleat. Note that the first and last folds are mountains.

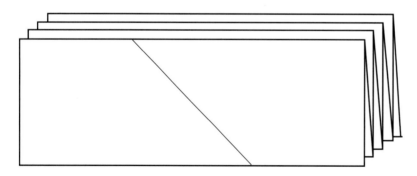

4.2.2_3
Concertina the folds, then make a 45-degree fold through all the layers. Note that the edge of the paper is at the bottom of the first pleat. Bend the new fold backwards and forwards to make it universal.

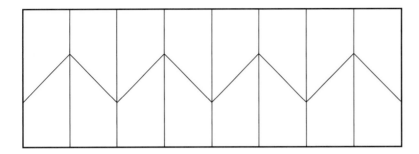

4.2.2_4
Open the concertina. This is the pattern.

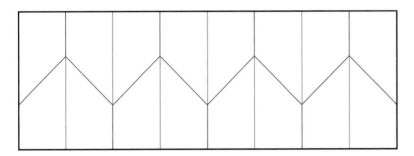

4.2.2_5
Carefully refold each crease exactly as shown, one at a time. Note that there are seven nodes and the zigzag is a continuous mountain fold. Each node is a meeting point for three mountain folds and one valley fold. When complete, the pleat will concertina up.

4.2.3   Rotational Gutters

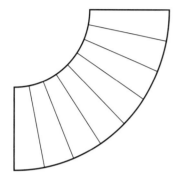

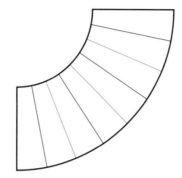

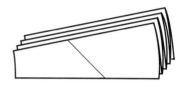

4.2.3_1
The linear V-pleat described previously will also work when the gutters are rotational. Here, a 90-degree arc is divided into eight accordion pleats, and the folds are all universal.

4.2.3_2
Refold the universal folds as a regular accordion pleat. Note that the first and last folds are mountains.

4.2.3_3
Concertina the folds, then make a 45-degree fold through all the layers. Note that the edge of the paper is at the bottom of the first pleat. Bend the new fold backwards and forwards to make it universal.

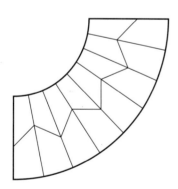

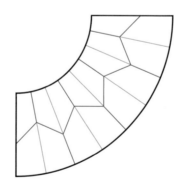

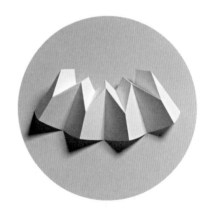

4.2.3_4
Open the concertina. This is the pattern.

4.2.3_5
Carefully refold each crease exactly as shown, one at a time. Note that there are seven nodes and the zigzag is a continuous mountain fold. Each node is a meeting point for three mountain folds and one valley fold. When complete, the pleat will concertina up.

Thin pieces of wood veneer were cut
precisely by laser and reassembled to create
this rigid, conical bowl form. The crease
pattern is similar to that on the facing page,
combined with the pattern on page 211.
Designed by Tine de Ruysser (Belgium).

4.2.4   Unequally Spaced Gutters

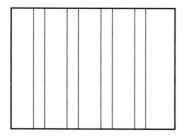

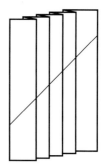

4.2.4_1
Create a basic knife pleat (see page 77).
Make each fold universal.

4.2.4_2
Refold the knife pleat, as shown.

4.2.4_3
Holding the pleats flat, carefully make an
angled fold through all the layers. Fold it
backwards and forwards to make it universal.

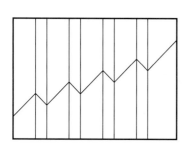

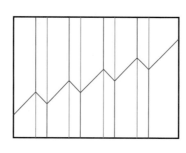

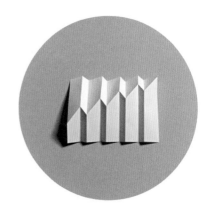

4.2.4_4
Open the paper to see this interesting
crease pattern!

4.2.4_5
As before, refold the universal folds so that
every node has three mountain folds and one
valley fold, and the zigzag is a continuous
mountain fold. When complete, the pleat
will concertina up.

4.3
Multiple Vs

Multiple Vs take the simple V made in the first section, above, and repeat it in a column. This simple technical idea creates many new opportunities for complex pleats, which will be further explored in later sections.

4.3.1   Concept

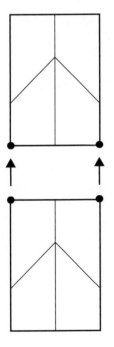
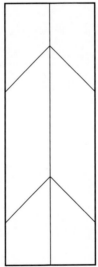
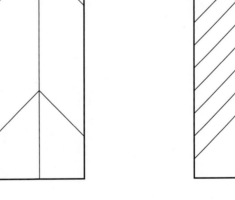
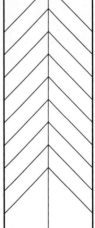

4.3.1_1
Two basic examples from the beginning of the chapter can be placed so that they touch bottom edge to top edge.

4.3.1_2
This is the result. The line of the join has disappeared, so that the sheet is continuous. Both Vs are on the same gutter.

4.3.1_3
Many Vs can be placed along the same gutter.

Intricate steel V-pleats support a 1.35-m-
(50-in-) long glass top 37cm (15in) above the
floor. Although at first glance the support
seems conventionally folded from a single
sheet, it is actually an intricate assembly
of many shaped pieces. Designed by Chris
Kabatsi/Arktura (USA).

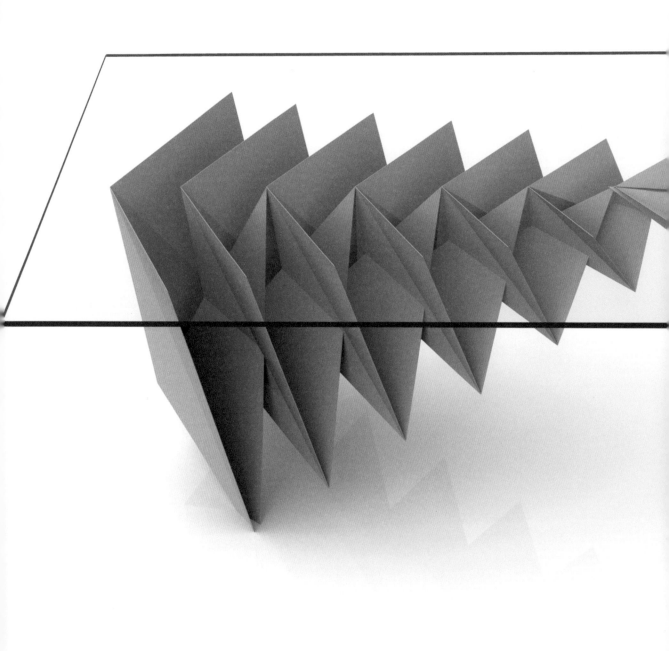

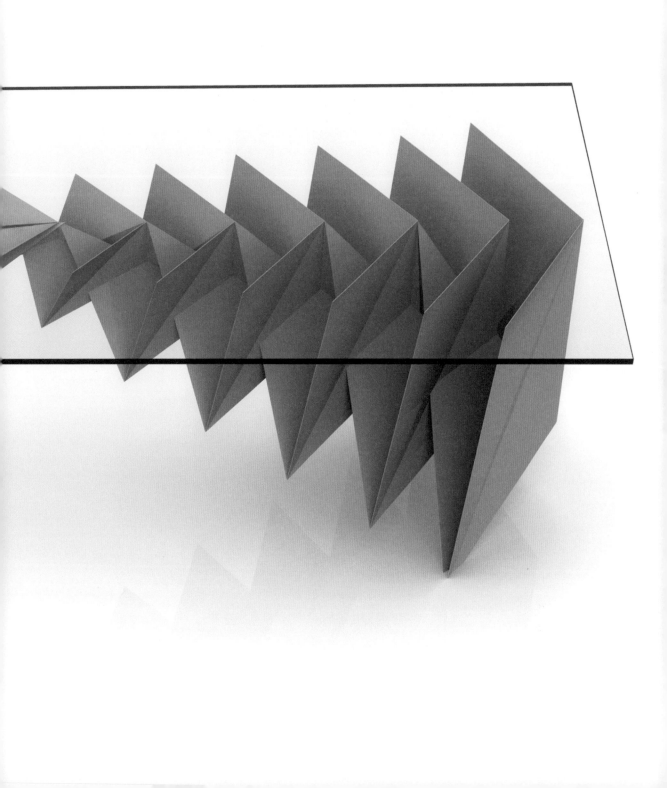

4.3.2   Basic Construction

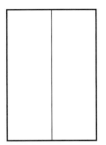

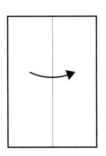

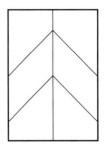

4.3.2_1
Create a universal fold down the centre line.

4.3.2_2
Fold in half.

4.3.2_3
Create two parallel universal folds at 45 degrees.

4.3.2_4
Unfold the paper. This is the result. The finished example is on the right in the photo. Note the mountain V and the valley V. (The example on the left shows the mountain V already formed, but the lower V has yet to be made.)

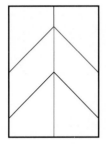 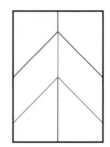

4.3.2_5
To create two V-pleats, first crease the paper to look like the left-hand drawing, ignoring the lower V. Then fold the lower V. Note that if the top V is a mountain, the bottom V will be the opposite fold, a valley. Note also how the gutter divides into three sections, mountain, valley and mountain.

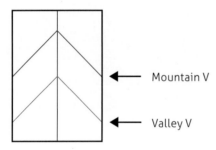

Mountain V

Valley V

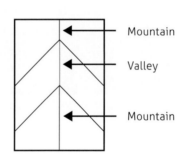

Mountain

Valley

Mountain

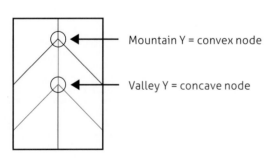

Mountain Y = convex node

Valley Y = concave node

4.3.2_6
The structure created by these two V-pleats is complex and worth analysing. There are three important points to note:

First, if one V-pleat is a mountain, the next will be a valley. Neighbouring V-pleats are always folded opposite ways (although there is a significant exception to this rule, as discussed in 'Vs in Opposition', page 201).

Second, at each node, the gutter will switch direction, from mountain to valley, or vice versa.

Third, a node where three mountain folds meet will always be *convex*. A node where three valley folds meet will always be *concave*.

Above
This unusual interpretation of a V-pleat uses
the pages of an existing book as its basic
material. By careful folding of the pages, the
contours of five V-pleats are revealed. The
text and the white borders create an extra
layer of pattern while the covers of the book
create a frame that is both structural and
visual. Designed by Eiko Ozawa (USA).

Below
Created on a knitting machine, this all-wool scarf features different densities of knit. When bunched up, the material wants to pleat along the less dense lines to create a dense mass of V-pleats. On the body, it creates an ever-changing mix of organic-looking open and closed V-pleats. Designed by Hadar Grizim, Department of Textile Design, Shenkar College, Tel Aviv (Israel).

4.3.3   Variations

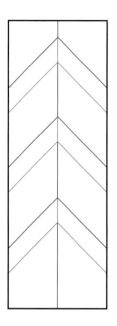

4.3.3_1
Here, the V-pleats are not equally spaced, but
progress down the gutter in the manner of a
knife pleat.

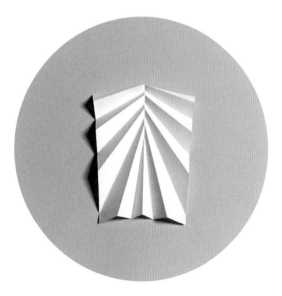

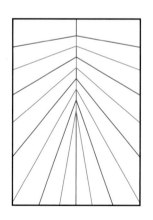

4.3.3_2
The V-pleats need not be parallel with
one another.

The circles above were originally created as the backdrop for a musical concert. They are made from a long rectangle of paper, the short side of which is the radius of the circle. The regular V-pleat grid is folded in, the short ends glued together to create a cylinder, then one end of the cylinder is gathered shut to form the centre of the final fan. In such a design, the key to success is to ensure that the rectangle is long enough to allow the cylinder to flatten. Designed by Anna Rudanski (Estonia).

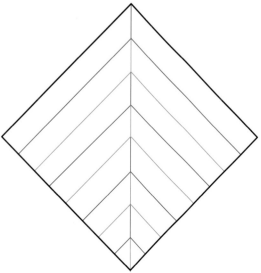

4.3.3_3
The gutter can run diagonally, so that
the pleats are parallel (or perpendicular)
to the edges.

4.4
Vs in Opposition

Vs in opposition are the troublemakers in the pleat family, disrupting an otherwise peaceful harmony of V-pleats. They introduce a new constructional rule, explained here, which needs to be understood if you intend to use V-pleats to their full potential. However, when understood, this technique will hugely increase their potential.

4.4.1   Concept

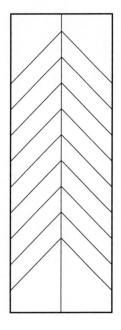

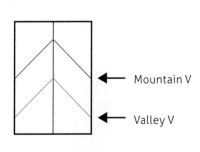

Mountain V

Valley V

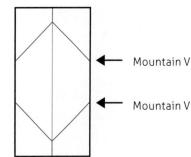

Mountain V

Mountain V

4.4.1_1
Let us remind ourselves how the V-pleats made in the previous section look. All the pleats are in line, one after another.

4.4.1_2
As we saw, when the pleats are in line, they alternate, mountain-valley ... etc.

4.4.1_3
However, when V-pleats are opposed, as they are here, they do not alternate mountain-valley. Instead, they remain the same fold. In this example, they are both mountains.

4.4.1_4
Note how the two V-pleats create a mirror image of each other here. The gutter fold that connects them is also the same fold (a mountain).

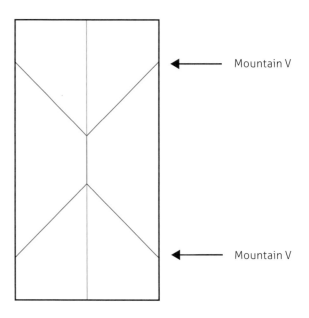

Mountain V

Mountain V

4.4.2 Basic Constructions

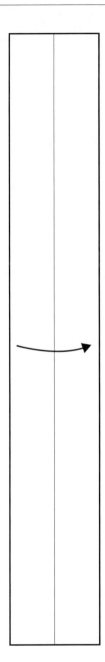

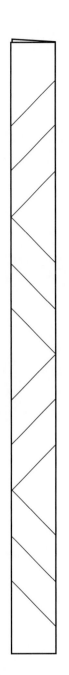

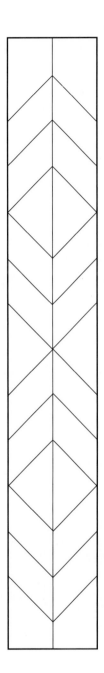

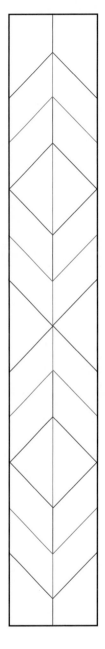

4.4.2_1
Having previously made the long centre fold universal, fold it in half.

4.4.2_2
Make a succession of 45-degree folds down the strip. In this example, three folds are in line, then the next three are a mirror of the previous three ... and so on. Make all the folds universal.

4.4.2_3
Open the strip. This is the pattern of folds.

4.4.2_4
Carefully refold the universal folds as mountains and valleys, exactly as described here. Note how when pleats are in line they alternate mountain-valley-mountain, but when one pleat is a mirror of the previous pleat, both pleats are mountains. (See photo overleaf.)

4.4.3   Variations

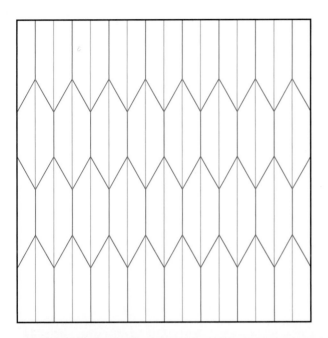

4.4.3_1
Here, every V-fold is a mirror of its neighbour on the same vertical gutter fold, so every V must be a mountain. The angles of the V-folds are at 60 degrees to the horizontal. If the angle is different, the canopy will arch either sooner or later.

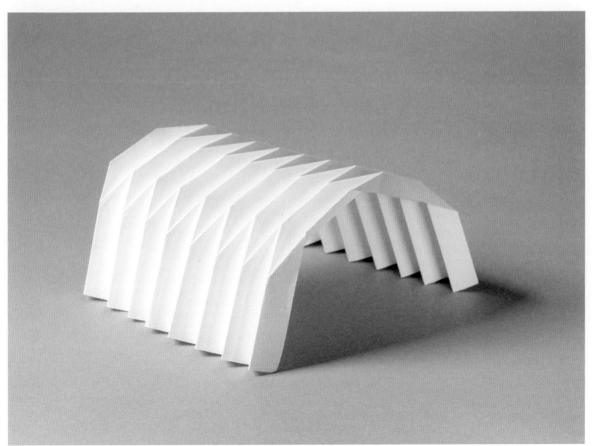

Made in aluminium and leather, this minimalist chair uses simple V-fold techniques to great effect. It is not a true folded sheet, but an assembly of V-forms that are joined in such a way as to add strength. The chair is one of several items of furniture in pleated aluminium designed by the same company, Four O Nine (China).

4.5
Multiple Gutters and Vs

Multiple gutters and Vs put together everything learnt so far in this chapter to create complex zigzag surfaces, all of which can be collapsed flat. This is the point in the book where the technically adventurous will acquire the tools to explore for evermore. Everyone will find their own technical limit.

4.5.1   Concept

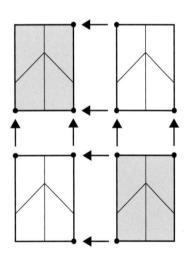

4.5.1_1
Here, four basic examples from the start of the chapter are placed together in a 2 x 2 grid. For ease of identification, alternate V-pleats are coloured grey.

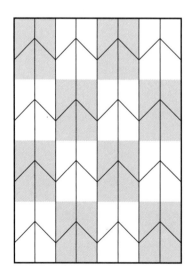

4.5.1_2
The grid can be further extended. Here the grid is 4 x 4, but it could extend to infinity.

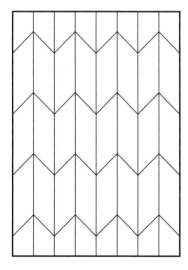

4.5.1_3
Removing the grey rectangles, the 4 x 4 grid now meshes into a seamless array of V-pleats.

4.5.2   Constructions

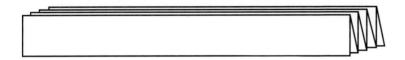

4.5.2_1
First divide a square into universal eighths,
then fold them into an accordion pleat.

4.5.2_2
Begin with the pleat made above. Create a
series of eight pleats, as shown. The odd
numbered pleats are at 45 degrees and the
even numbered pleats are at 60 degrees.
Make all the folds universal, then carefully
collapse them, observing all the mountain-
valley rules explained so far in this chapter.

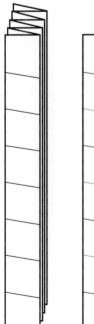

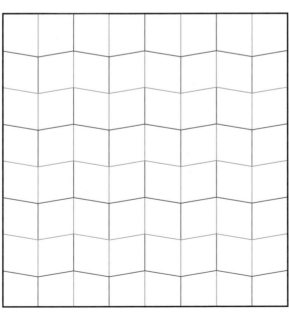

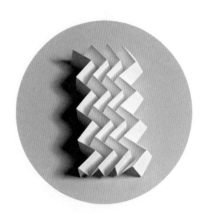

4.5.2_3
Here, the V-pleats are almost straight, enabling
the sheet to concertina up very small.

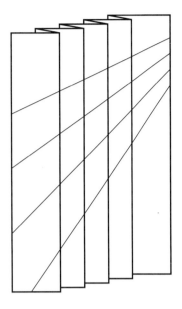

4.5.2_4
In this example, knife pleats are crossed by a series of angled folds. For clarity, the drawing exaggerates the top edge of the knife pleat.

4.5.2_5
This flatter drawing shows how the surface will actually look.

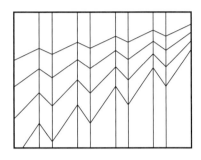

4.5.2_6
When the knife pleats are opened, a series of converging zigzags will be seen.

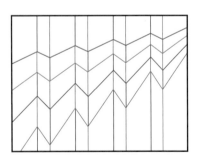

4.5.2_7
Refold the universal folds as shown. Note how adjacent zigzags are always mountain-valley opposites.

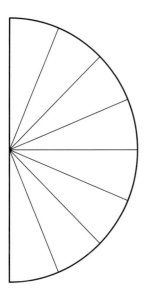

4.5.2_8
The construction will also work with
rotational pleats.

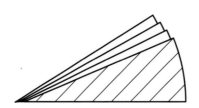

4.5.2_9
Here, a half-circle is pleated into eighths, and
a series of parallel V-folds are placed across
at an angle.

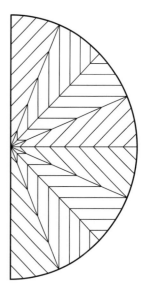

4.5.2_10
When unfolded, this is the pattern.

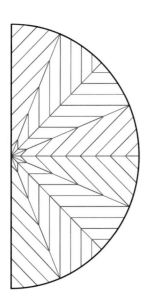

4.5.2_11
Refold the universal folds as shown,
starting with the largest zigzag and finishing
with the smallest.

Made in ceramic by the casting technique, this design is one of a number of similar vases, bowls and pots from the same manufacturer that make decorative use of the V-pleat. The precision of the casting ensures that the folded edges remain sharp, and that the piece retains much of the crispness of the paper form it mimics. Designed by Bloomingville.

4.5.3   Shaped Sheets

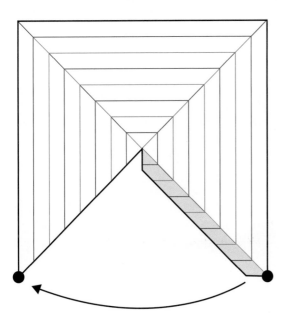

4.5.3_1
An interesting way to create a series of
concentric V-pleats is to think of a polygon
– in this example, a square – and to remove
one side (but leaving a narrow glue tab).
When folded up, the square becomes an
equilateral triangle.

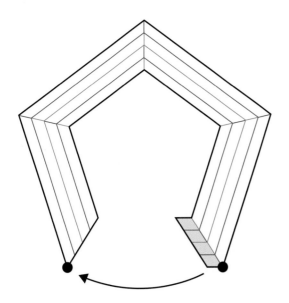

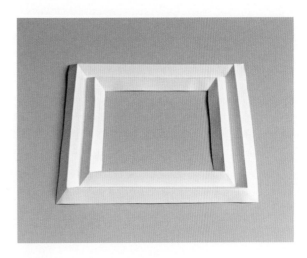

4.5.3_2
Similarly, a pentagon when folded up will
create a concentrically pleated square. If the
hole in the centre is enlarged, the pleated
square makes a very effective frame. With
a little adaptation, the frame can become
rectangular, not square.

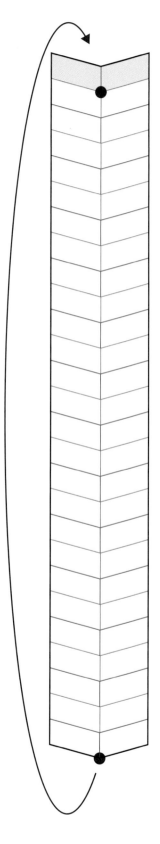

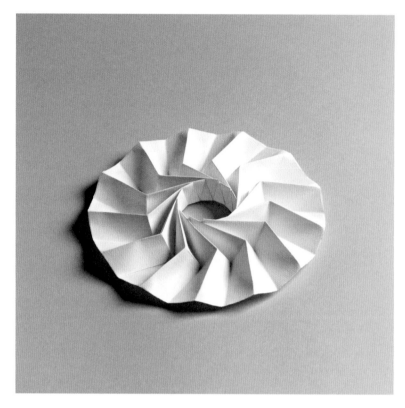

4.5.3_3
A series of large-angled V-pleats when glued into a ring can be flattened so that one edge of the ring becomes the outer perimeter of a disc, and the other edge squashes together at the centre point. The result is a very dynamic circular zigzag.

Opposite page
This temporary Chapel of St Loup was built from wood, with folded steel plates along the folds to which the wood is screwed. The different facets were pre-fabricated in a factory and assembled on site in ten days. Dimensions: 19 x 12 x 7m (61 x 39 x 23ft). Designed by Localarchitecture (Switzerland).

4.6

Concertina Boxes

Concertina boxes are practical, fun and beautiful. Like all V-pleat structures, they can be collapsed flat or stretched open – even bent to one side to create an arch. There are two different forms of concertina box, both described here.

4.6.1   Chamfered Corners

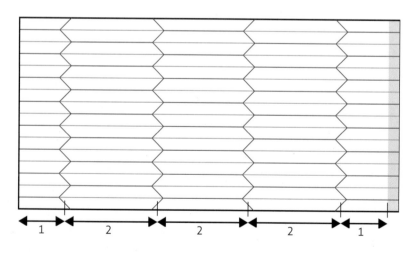

4.6.1_1
The simplest concertina box has corners of 90 degrees, so the box is square. To achieve this, the zigzag folds must be exactly at 45 degrees. It is important to close the box with a glue line that is not at a corner, but in the middle of a side. In this way, each corner will be only one layer thick and they will all stretch or compress equally.

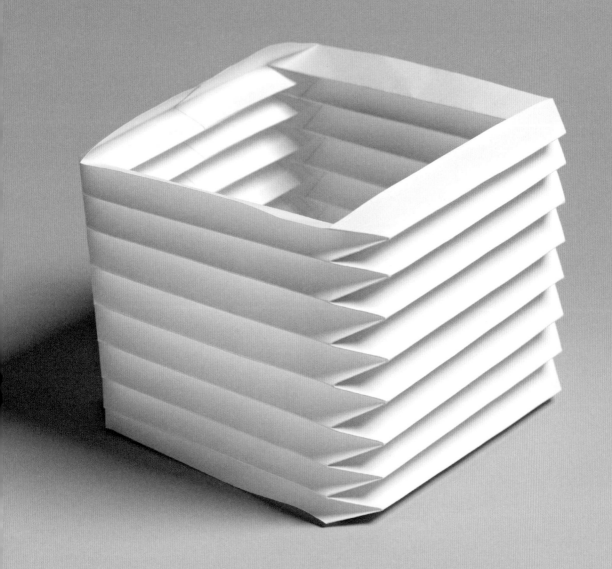

4.6.2 Variations

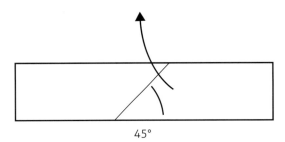

45°

4.6.2_1
If an angle of 45 degrees is made
across a line of accordion pleats, like this …

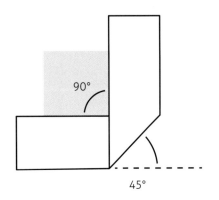

90°

45°

4.6.2_2
… the interior angle will become 90 degrees.
Thus, the angle is suitable for a box with
90-degree corners.

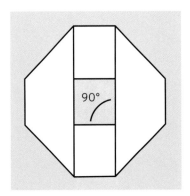

90°

4.6.2_3
Repeated four times along the strip and the
ends glued together, as in the previous
section, the box will be square or
rectangular.

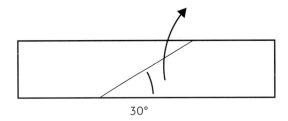

30°

4.6.2_4
If the angle is made at 30 degrees …

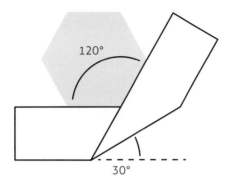

4.6.2_5
... this will create an interior angle of 120 degrees, suitable for making a hexagonal concertina box ...

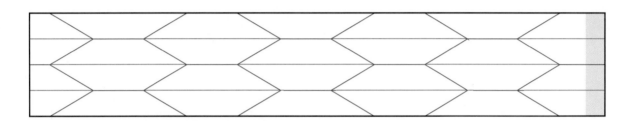

4.6.2_6
... like this. Note how the six zigzags are all 30 degrees to the horizontal.

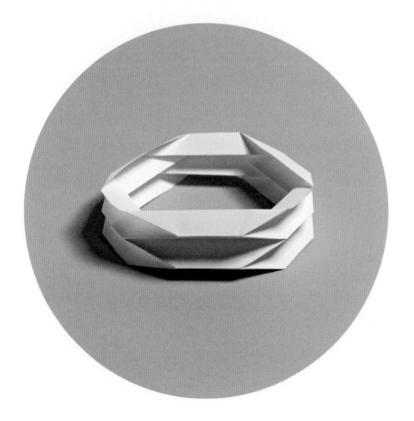

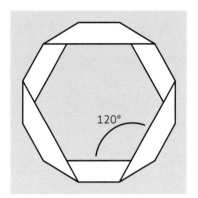

4.6.2_7
This is how a hexagonal concertina box will look in plan view.

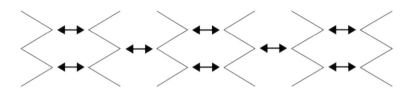

4.6.2_8
Here are the six zigzag V-pleats, isolated from the remainder of the crease pattern. Note the arrowed corners. These corners can be brought ever closer together until they touch ...

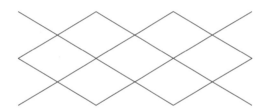

4.6.2_9
... like this, to create a lattice of criss-crossing V-pleats.

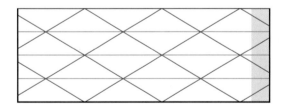

4.6.2_10
When the horizontal folds are reintroduced, the mountain folds connecting the zigzags have been eliminated, to leave this simple pattern of horizontal valleys.

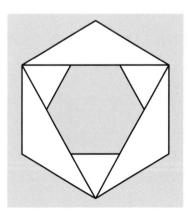

4.6.2_11
This is how the box will look in plan view. Although the space in the centre and the outer perimeter are both still hexagons, the opening has become a triangle. Thus, although the box has the appearance of using triangular geometry, the geometry is hexagonal.

The same bringing together of the zigzag corners to create a simplified lattice can be used with any even-sided polygon.

4.6.3   Square Corners

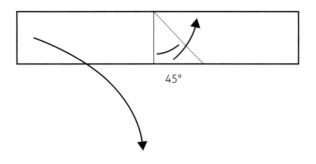

4.6.3_1
In this second type of pattern, a vertical mountain fold is paired with an angled valley fold. The angle between them determines the number of sides of the box.

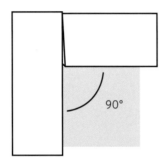

4.6.3_2
An angle between the folds of 45 degrees will create an interior angle of 90 degrees.

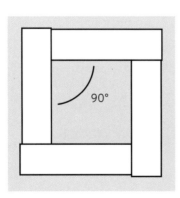

4.6.3_3
If this pattern is repeated a total of four times, the box will be square.

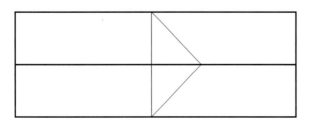

4.6.3_4
Using this principle, it is now possible to develop a complete crease pattern. First, mirror the two folds, so that the angled valley becomes a side-on V.

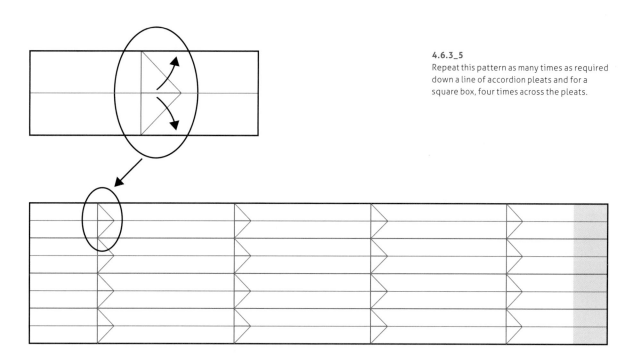

4.6.3_5
Repeat this pattern as many times as required down a line of accordion pleats and for a square box, four times across the pleats.

4.6.4   Variations

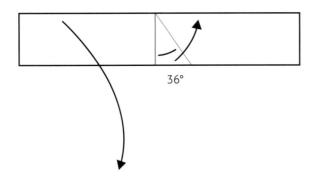

36°

4.6.4_1
If the angle between the vertical mountain and the sloping valley is changed to 36 degrees …

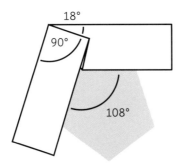

18°

90°

108°

4.6.4_2
… the interior angle becomes 108 degrees, which is the angle needed to create a pentagonal box. Note that the exterior angle is also 108 degrees, created by adding together 90 and 18 degrees; 18 degrees is the remainder from 90 degrees when 36 degrees is folded over on itself: $90 - (36 + 36) = 18$.

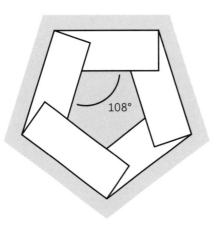

108°

4.6.4_3
This is the plan view of the complete pentagonal box.

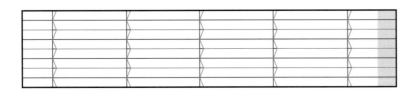

4.6.4_4
The complete crease pattern has five vertical lines. Whereas the angle between the vertical mountain fold and the zigzag valley is critical, the number of horizontal folds (the accordion pleat) is variable.

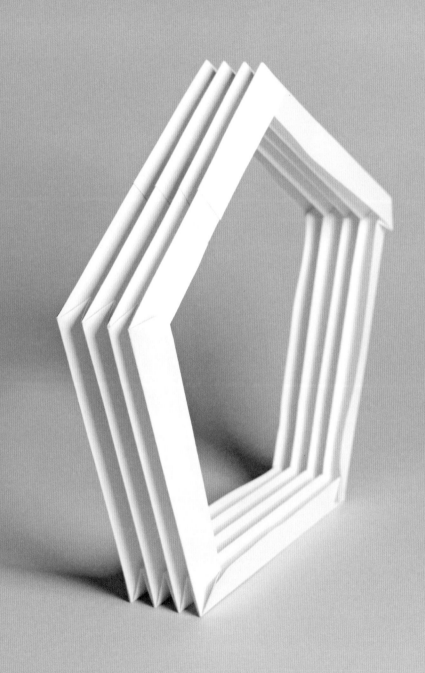

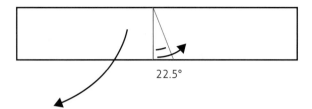

4.6.4_5
The same construction principle can be used to create a box with any number of sides. In this example, the angle between the vertical mountain and the angled valley is 22.5 degrees.

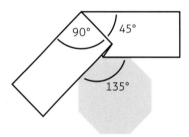

4.6.4_6
This angle will create an interior angle of 135 degrees, which is the angle needed to create an octagon.

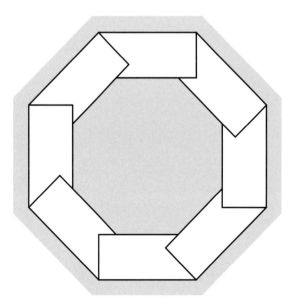

4.6.4_7
Here is the plan view of the complete octagonal box.

Made from Tyvek®, a paper-like plastic
sheet with good folding properties but
which is difficult to rip, the three pieces
shown here can open and collapse as
the wearer playfully reacts to changing
circumstances. Designed by Jule Waibel (UK).

5

WORKING WITH GRIDS

Working With Grids

Grids are fascinating elastic surfaces that can be as simple or as complicated as you choose. They make extensive use of the V-pleat, so before beginning to work from this chapter, you are advised to work through the previous chapter with some diligence.

Making grids can be a slow and exacting process, but once made, many interesting pleat patterns can be created, changed and remade in a prolonged period of reinvention, all with the same sheet.

Familiarity with how to divide a sheet is essential, so before beginning, you may wish to reacquaint yourself with Chapter 1:

'Dividing Paper' (see page 22). With only a little practice, your making of grids will become quicker and – perhaps paradoxically – also more accurate, so it is worth labouring through the construction of your first few grids to achieve the fluency that awaits. Work is always rewarded.

This chapter begins by exploring the possibilities offered by folding square grids, followed by the more esoteric possibilities of less familiar triangular grids. If you are looking for an area of pleating to explore where few have explored before, working from triangular grids is for you.

5.1
Square Grids

Square grids are simpler to make than the triangular grids that follow; we are all very familiar with angles of 90 and 45 degrees, so the geometry is comfortable for us. The key to success is to fold the grids carefully.

5.1.1   Making the Grid

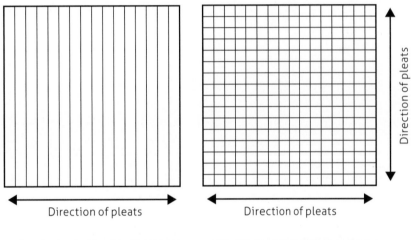

Direction of pleats

Direction of pleats

Direction of pleats

5.1.1_1
A square grid is the overlaying of two or more lines of pleats at a 90-degree angle. The most common grid features the overlapping of two sets of pleats parallel to the edges.

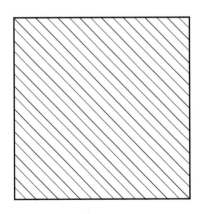

5.1.1_2
However, the grid may also lie at 45 degrees to the edges ...

5.1.1_3
... like this.

5.1.1_4
The most common grid sees the overlaying of a third line of pleats, parallel to the edge. The folds in this line of pleats are universal.

5.1.2   How to Collapse the Full Grid

5.1.2_1
This is the full, collapsed grid of zigzags.
The following series of photographs explains
how to create it from the grid.

How to Collapse the Grid

5.1.2_2
Crease the 15 vertical lines of symmetry to make a simple accordion pleat. Hold the creased paper symmetrically as shown, thumbs on the front and fingers on the back.

5.1.2_3
Use your fingers and thumbs to pop and press a double row of zigzags. The upper line is a mountain zigzag; the lower line is a valley zigzag. Use existing mountain and valley folds to find these folds.

You do not need to invent any new folds!
Work across the paper from edge to edge, opening only that part of the paper where you are working. The remainder of the paper can be concertinaed closed.

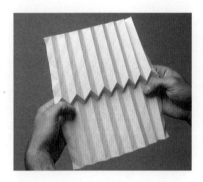

5.1.2_4
This is the double row of zigzags, completed. It can take some time to acquire the knack of how to make them.

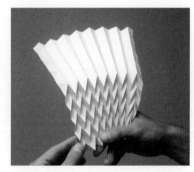

5.1.2_5
Continue to make double rows of zigzags until you reach the bottom edge of the paper.

5.1.2_6
Go back to the middle of the paper and work upwards, creating more double rows of zigzags until the top edge is reached.

5.1.2_7
Collapse the paper into a very narrow, thick stick. Press it flat to sharpen all the folds.

5.1.2_8
Now pull open the stick to reveal the zigzags inside.

This huge multi-V-grid ceiling was made from hundreds of parallelograms of corrugated cardboard and suspended above a concert-going audience. A complex manually-operated lever system above it enabled different sections of the ceiling to rise and fall dramatically like a swelling sea, in reaction to the music. Dimensions: 25m x 11m (81ft x 36ft). Designed by Anna Kubelik (Germany).

5.1.3   Less-than-full Variations

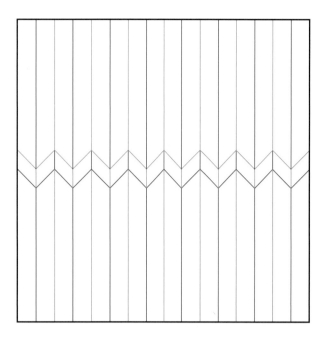

5.1.3_1
Eliminate some of the zigzags

A few, or many – or almost all (as shown here) – of the zigzags can be removed from the grid. Here, just a mountain-valley pairing of zigzags remain.

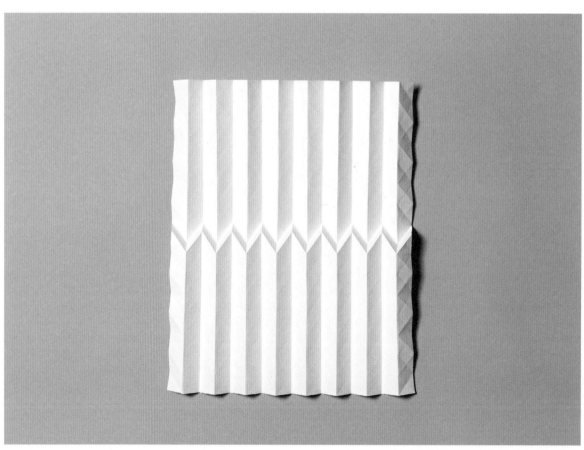

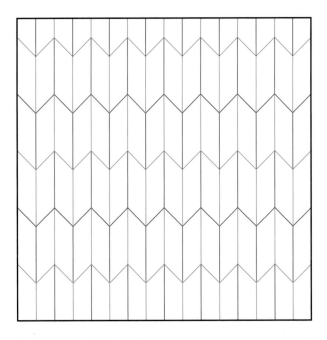

5.1.3_2
Space out the zigzags

The zigzags need not be packed tightly together, but can be spaced out, a little or a lot.

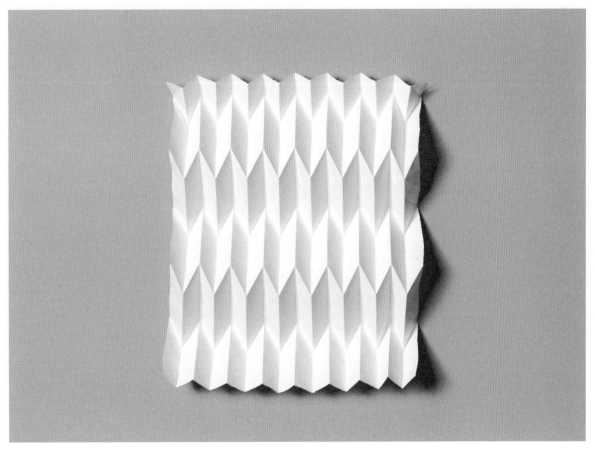

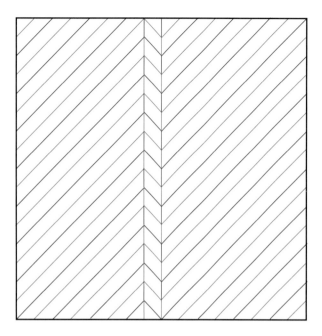

5.1.3_3
Reduce the number of accordion pleats

A few or many of the vertical accordion pleats can be removed, so that the zigzags continue for long distances across the grid.

5.1.3_4
Space the accordion pleats irregularly

In this example, five accordion pleats are followed by three that are missing. The effect is an appealing mix of visual rhythms.

5.1.3_5
*Reduce both the number of accordion pleats
and zigzags*

By reducing the number of both elements in
the grid, a complex intermixing of accordion
and zigzag rhythms becomes possible.

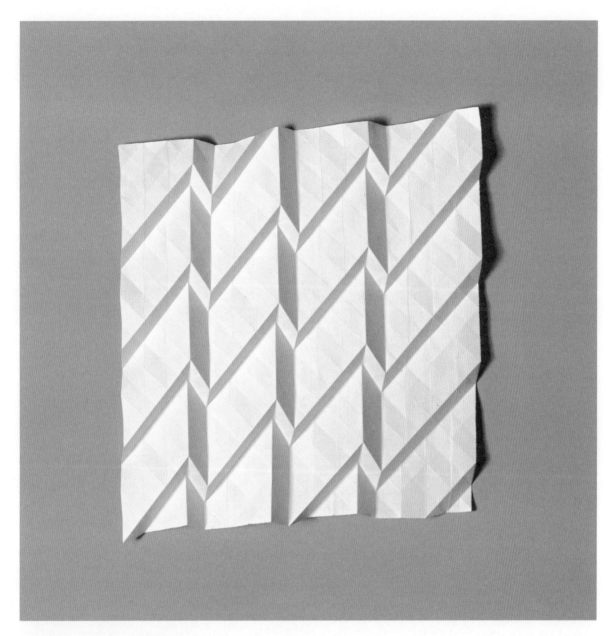

Considered separately or in combination,
the five suggestions above for reducing
the fully collapsed grid will create a whole
constellation of pleated surfaces and forms
– enough to fill a book. Some of the concepts
and the technical finesse necessary to make
them are quite advanced, but if you are
motivated and patient, time spent on this
topic will eventually be richly rewarded.

These photographs were taken by a student as part of a design project to document her self-initiated folding experiments. Over a semester she printed and collected in her notebook more than 100 photographs, experimenting freely with lighting, colour, texture and surface graphics. As a collection – of which only a small part is reproduced here – they form an invaluable resource for future work. Designed by Janine Farber, overseas student, Department of Fashion Design, Shenkar College, Tel Aviv (Israel).

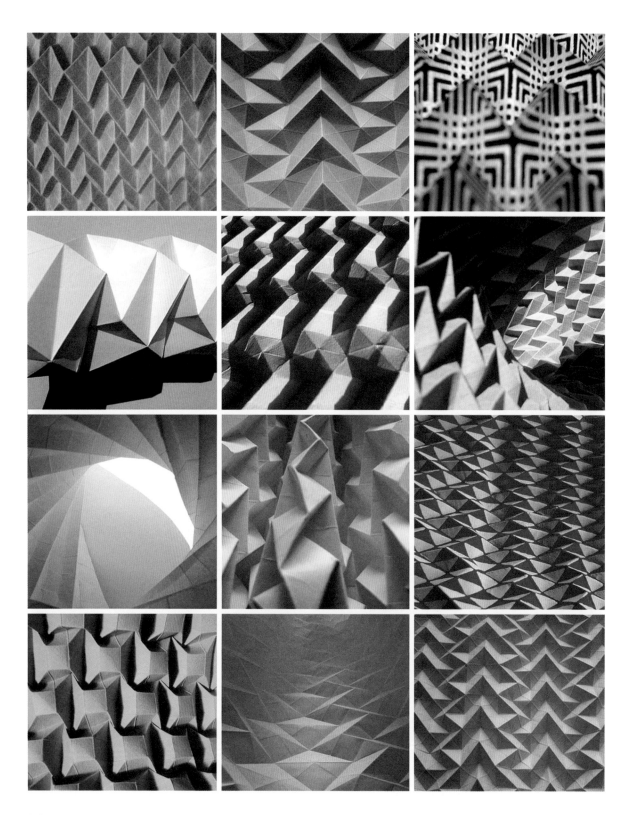

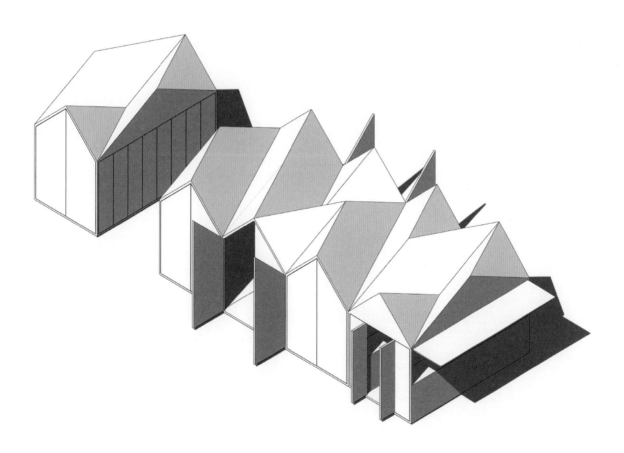

Created as a competition entry to design a series of connected or disconnected small cabins, this ingenious roof system is visible at street level as a series of traditional gable ends. From above the roof level, a series of complex multi-V-pleat surfaces are visible that can connect in many semi-random combinations. Designed by K.W.Y. (Germany).

5.2
Triangular Grids

Triangular grids are counterintuitive and, for that reason, little used. We are very unfamiliar with the concept of using triangular geometry, but it is as productive as the square geometry used in the previous section.

5.2_1
This is the triangular grid made previously in 'Sixty-degree Grids' (see page 47).

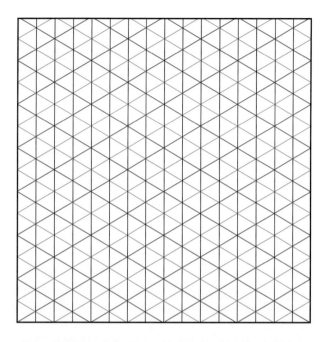

5.2_2
To create an accordion pleat, add mountains between the valleys on the two sets of sloping folds. See 'Pleated Sixteenths' (page 30) for tips on how to create an accordion pleat from a line of valley folds. Also subdivide the vertical line of pleats, turning all the vertical folds into universal folds. In this example, the paper was cut square, but this is not essential.

Any of the pleated surfaces made in the previous section on square grids can now be made with this triangular grid. The effect is to create V-pleats that are wider than V-pleats at 45 degrees.

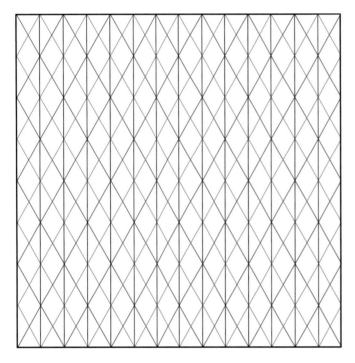

5.2_3
An interesting alternative is to create the
two lines of sloping accordion pleats in
the previous step, then to turn the paper
90 degrees and add the verticals. Rotating
the sheet in this way creates sloping folds
that are 60 degrees to the horizontal,
whereas in the previous step, they were
only 30 degrees to the horizontal. Curiously,
on a square, the paper will only divide into
14 verticals, not 16.

With this grid, the V-pleats become very
tight. As before, this alternative grid can
make anything that a square grid can make.

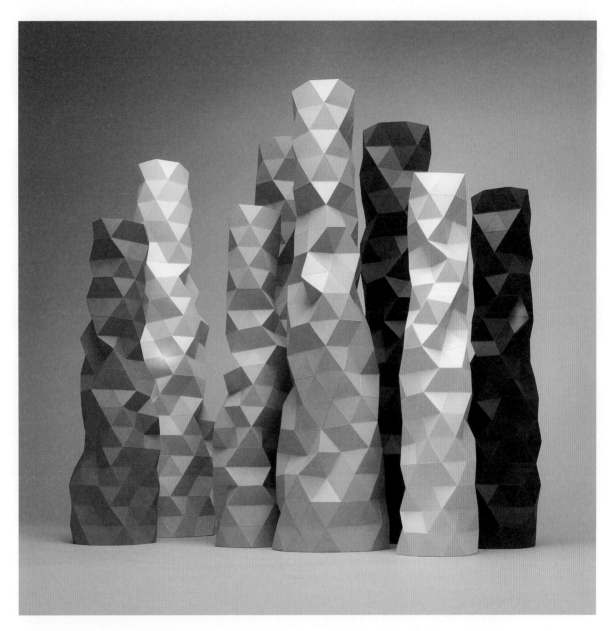

Opposite
A conventional photographic print was
divided into a 60-degree grid, digitally
manipulated so that the colours occasionally
followed the grid lines, then printed, folded
on the grid and geometrically crumpled.
The effect is both playful and disturbing.
Dimensions: 70 x 53 x 23cm (28 x 21 x 9in).
Designed by Andrea Russo (Italy).

Above
These vases are created by casting
water-based resin into a hand-made mould.
This low-tech method creates a result with
pleasingly crisp edges and a machine-made
aesthetic. Height: approximately 40cm
(16in). Designed by Phil Cuttance (UK).

6

PLEATS LAID ACROSS PLEATS

Pleats Laid
Across Pleats

This final technical chapter collects together everything learnt so far, to present several ways of laying one line of pleats perpendicularly across another to create intricate surfaces and forms. It is fascinating to see how two lines can interweave or interact to create a result that is always surprising, beautiful and more than the sum of its parts.

The four methods shown here are just a few of many. If you wish to explore for yourself, take any two pleat patterns from this book and lay the first line perpendicularly over the second line. Now try again, but this time laying the second over the first line. See how you can make the two lines work together – there are often many different ways. To save time, always explore with small grids, made by dividing the paper into four or eight. If something looks to be working, make it again from a grid of 16 or 32 – even more. You can even turn overlaying into an extreme sport by trying to overlay three lines using the triangular grid described in the previous chapter.

6.1
Knife
Across Knife

A line of knife pleats laid perpendicularly across another line of knife pleats may not sound very promising, but if the two lines of pleats are knitted together in a specific way, the results are spectacular. This section also shows some of the many ways in which one knitted line can develop into many.

6.1.1   Basic Example

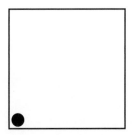

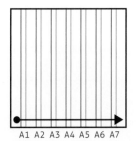

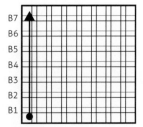

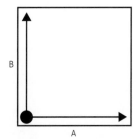

6.1.1_1
In the bottom left-hand corner of a square, mark a circle. (The mark here is large, so it can be easily seen, but a simple small dot is sufficient.)

6.1.1_2
Create a series of knife pleats, which begin at the dot. This is the 'A' line of knife pleats. Make them in the order A1 to A7.

6.1.1_3
Similarly, create a second line of knife pleats that also begin at the dot. This is the 'B' line, made in the order B1 to B7.

6.1.1_4
To summarize, two lines of knife pleats have been created – A and B – both of which have their origin at the dotted corner.

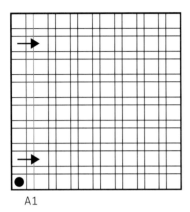

A1

6.1.1_5
We can now begin to collapse the two lines of pleats, beginning at the dot. First, make just the knife pleat A1.

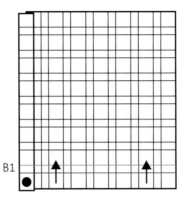

B1

6.1.1_6
Hold the A1 pleat flat. Now, make just the knife pleat B1, folding it on top of the A1 pleat.

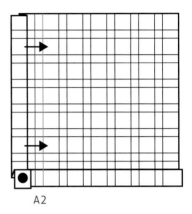

A2

6.1.1_7
Hold the B1 pleat flat. Now, make the A2 pleat.

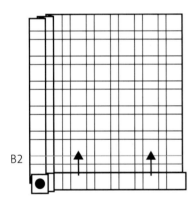

B2

6.1.1_8
Hold the A2 pleat flat. Now, make the B2 pleat. Continue this sequence of pleats across the surface. The next pleat will be A3, then B3, A4, B4, A5, B5, A6, B6, A7 and finally B7. It is crucial to keep alternating between the two lines of pleats, so that they knit together symmetrically.

A B C D E
F G H I J K
L M N O P
Q R S T U
V W X Y Z

Left
To make this script the finished example on the facing page was folded in paper, then a letterform was carefully painted onto the different layers. As the layers stretched and separated, white spaces were introduced into the depiction of the letter. A photograph was taken of each 'broken' letterform, then manipulated with CAD. After 26 repetitions with different letters, a full alphabet of the typeface was created. Designed by Alexandra Wilhelm. Overseas student project, Department of Communication Design, Shenkar College, Tel Aviv (Israel).

Right
A few horizontal and vertical knife pleats were created in a sheer fabric, so that different tones would contrast against a dark under-slip. Some of the pleats also twist (as described on page 116). The front is held together with a black zip. Designed by Ohad Krief, student project, Department of Fashion Design, Shenkar College, Tel Aviv (Israel).

255

6.1.2   Diagonal Variation

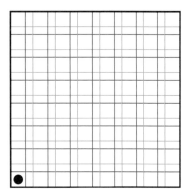

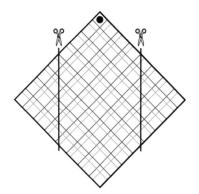

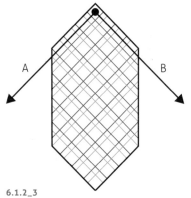

6.1.2_1
Create a copy of the knife pleat grid made previously. Note the dot corner and that all the folds are parallel to the edges.

6.1.2_2
The crease pattern can be rotated through 45 degrees so that the dot corner is now at the top. Connect the mid-points of two pairs of the edges with two cuts.

6.1.2_3
This is the result. Crucially, the two lines of knife pleats, A and B, still exist and can be knitted together in the manner described on page 254.

The knife-across-knife technique is taken to an extreme level of technical complexity to create a piece that has a remarkably organic aesthetic. Made originally in paper, it was later cast in bronze and entitled 'Cliff'. Height: 45cm (18in). Designed by Goran Konjevod (USA).

Folded from almost transparent *tengujo-shi*
paper, these 25 pieces were created to put on
the covers of a series of scholarly magazines
devoted to origami research. Their
informality contrasts sharply with the
measured pleats found elsewhere
in the book. Dimensions when folded:
approximately 75 x 75mm (3 x 3in).
Designed by Goran Konjevod (USA).

6.1.3   Three Lines of Knife Pleats

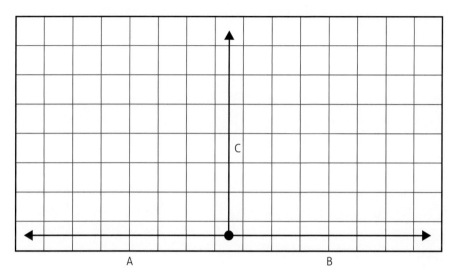

6.1.3_1
Divide half a square into an 8 x 15 grid
(the simplest way to do this is to divide
into a simple 8 x 16 grid and then cut off one
division along adjacent edges). The 'point of
origin' dot that was previously in a corner is
now in the middle of the bottom edge. Three
lines of knife pleats can have their points of
origin at this place – A, B and C.

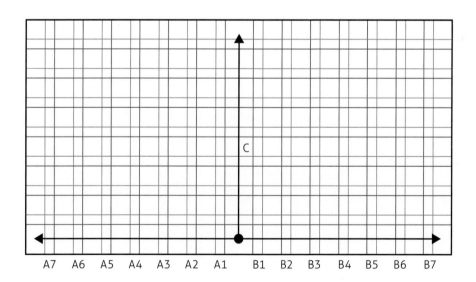

6.1.3_2
Begin with the A line of knife pleats, creating
first A1 and finally A7 at the left-hand edge.
Similarly, create line B, creating first B1 and
finally B7 at the right-hand edge.

6.1.3_3

Finally, create the C line of knife pleats. Begin – as always – at the dot and make pleat C1, which will stretch from one edge of the sheet to the other. Continue up the sheet, finishing with C7, near the top edge.

The three lines of pleats may now be knitted together. The cycle is:

A1-B1-C1
A2-B2-C2
A3-B3-C3
A4-B4-C4
A5-B5-C5
A6-B6-C6
A7-B7-C7

Be careful to follow this sequence in strict order. The result will resemble half a pyramid.

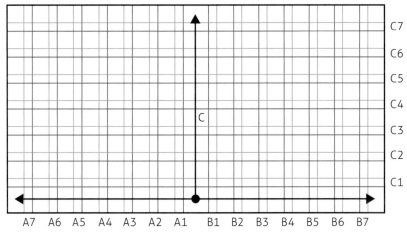

6.1.4   Four and More Lines of Knife Pleats

6.1.4_1

Divide a square into a 16 x 16 grid of mountains, then cut off one division along two adjacent edges to leave a 15 x 15 grid. This odd-numbered grid means that the dot will now sit in a square in the centre of the paper. If the grid was 16 x 16, it would sit – incorrectly – on an intersection of two folds. With the dot in the centre, it is now possible to create four lines of knife pleats with their origins at the dot: A, B, C and D.

Note how each line begins with a 1 (A1, B1, C1, D1) and ends with a 7 (A7, B7, C7, D7). Make each line of pleats individually. When they are made, knit them together in the sequence:

A1-B1-C1-D1
A2-B2-C2-D2
... and so on, until
A7-B7-C7-D7
The result will resemble a stepped pyramid. By massaging and expanding the pyramid from the inside, the pyramid will double or treble its height.

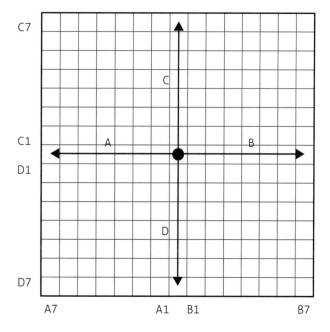

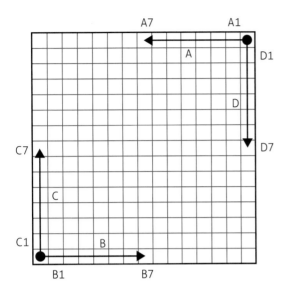

6.1.4_2

In some ways, this example can be considered the opposite of the previous example. The grid is 15 x 15. There are now two dots, in opposite corners. Knife pleat lines A and D originate from the dot in the top right-hand corner, and lines B and C from the dot in the lower left-hand corner. Each line creates seven knife pleats that meet at the centre point of the sheet.

As before, make each knife pleat line separately, then knit them together in the familiar way:

A1-B1-C1-D1
A2-B2-C2-D2
...and so on to
A7-B7-C7-D7
The result wll resemble an inverted table.

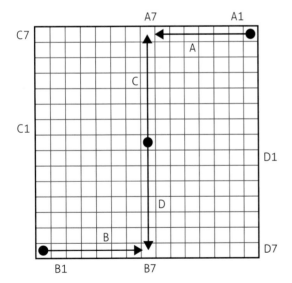

6.1.4_3

This example combines the previous two. Now there are three dots and the grid is 15 x 15. Knife pleat lines A and B originate from the dots in the corners, and lines C and D from the single dot in the middle.

As before, make each line separately, then knit them together in the order described above. The result will resemble two halves of a stepped pyramid.

6.1.4_4
There is no limit to the number of knife pleat
lines that can be knitted together. In this
example there are six, though A and B are
each repeated twice.

Look closely and it becomes clear that the
structure is simply 6.1.4_1, repeated twice.
Since all the pleats on all the structures in
this section meet the edge of the sheet at
90 degrees, it is possible to join sheets
together, providing the pleats match across
the join. Once this is understood, it becomes
possible to make a huge number of knife
pleat arrays that are knitted together in a
huge number of combinations, depending
where the dots are sited. The result will
resemble two stepped pyramids.

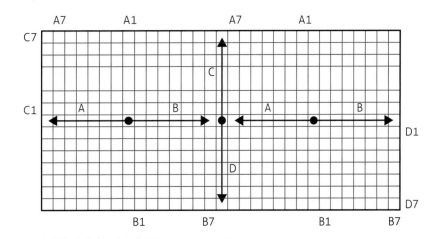

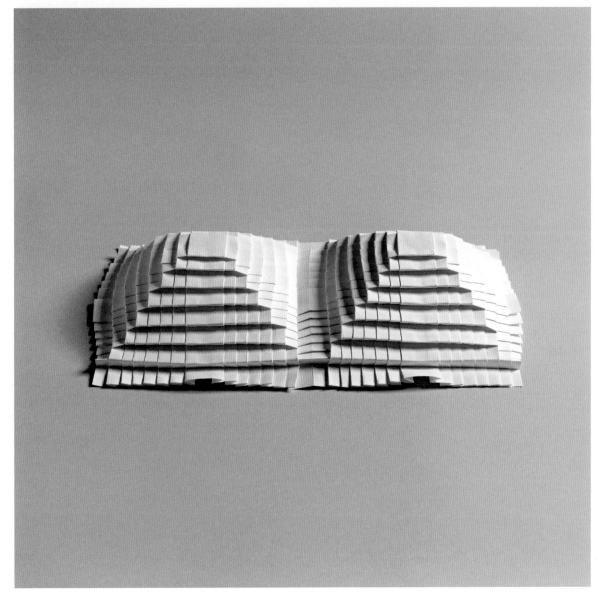

6.2

Accordion Across Knife

A line of accordion pleats laid perpendicularly across a line of knife pleats has the potential to create curved forms. The technique shown in the photographic sequence of lifting one knife pleat up from the one underneath is simple, but if repeated many times will create forms of great beauty.

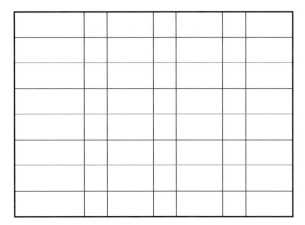

6.2_1
Create three simple knife pleats.

6.2_2
Unfold the pleats and make an accordion pleat into eighths. Note that the first and last folds are both mountains.

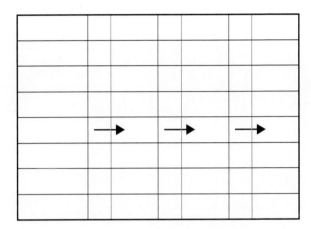

6.2_3
Refold the knife pleats.

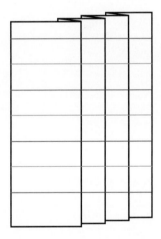

6.2_4
Refold the accordion pleats.

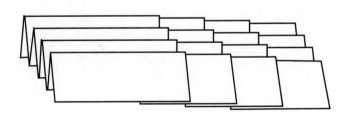

6.2_5
This is the basic array. The number of both knife pleats and accordion pleats can increase greatly.

How to Pull the Pleats Open

6.2_6
Hold the paper the same way around as
Step 5, with the bottom row of knife pleats
on the right. Hold as shown.

6.2_7
Grip the paper firmly with your left hand
and swivel the paper in your right hand
downwards by 15 to 20 degrees.

6.2_8
Repeat the previous step with the next
square, travelling down the right-hand
edge of the paper.

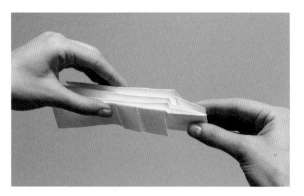

6.2_9
Repeat twice more to complete the row,
then gather all the pleats together.

6.2_10
This is the result. The squares on the right
appear to have dropped out of line. Squash
the paper firmly flat to establish new creases.

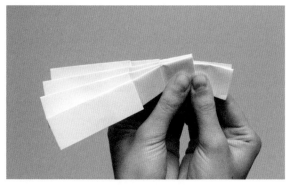

6.2_11
Repeat Steps 7 and 8 with the next row,
creating four new swivels of 15 to 20 degrees.

6.2_12
This is the result. As before, squash the paper flat in order to establish new creases.

6.2_13
Repeat the previous steps twice more on the two remaining lines of pleats. The paper will be seen to curve gradually.

The bowl features a series of accordion across knife pleats, explained on the previous spreads. The pleats are made on a cylinder of paper, coloured with pastel. Extra folding closes one end of the cylinder to create the base, while the other end is folded only half-closed. The design is not cut, only folded. Diameter: 30cm (12in). Designed by Paul Jackson (UK).

Similar in construction to the piece on the facing page, but technically more complex, this life-size rendition of a car tyre is titled 'Swerve Off'. Note the intricate way in which the tread of the tyre is created. The whole piece is folded from one uncut sheet of paper. Designed by Etienne Cliquet (France).

6.3
Upright
Across Upright

A line of upright pleats laid perpendicularly across another line of upright pleats will create a series of boxed compartments. A little experimentation with the heights of the pleats and the distance between them will yield many interesting variations.

6.3_1
Create six upright pleats, with the mountain folds on the middle and quarter lines.

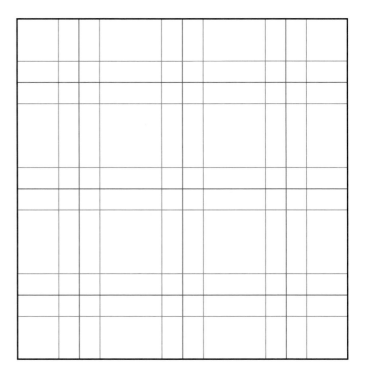

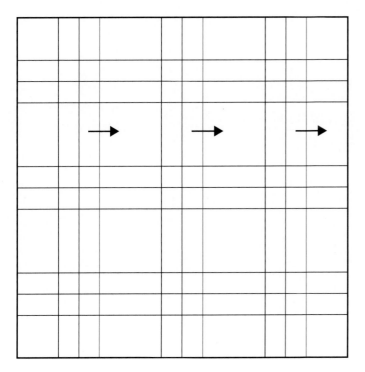

6.3_2
Refold the three vertical upright pleats, but as if they are knife pleats, allowing them to flatten towards the right.

6.3_3
Now, make the three horizontal upright pleats.

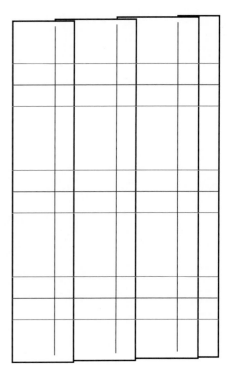

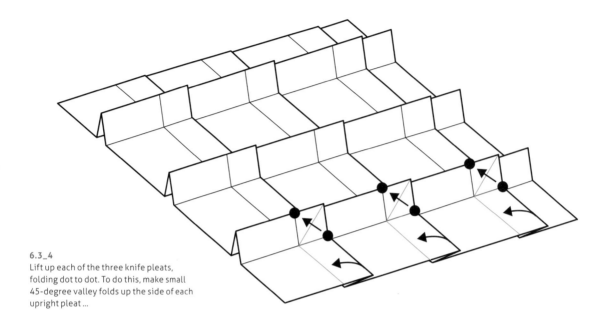

6.3_4
Lift up each of the three knife pleats,
folding dot to dot. To do this, make small
45-degree valley folds up the side of each
upright pleat …

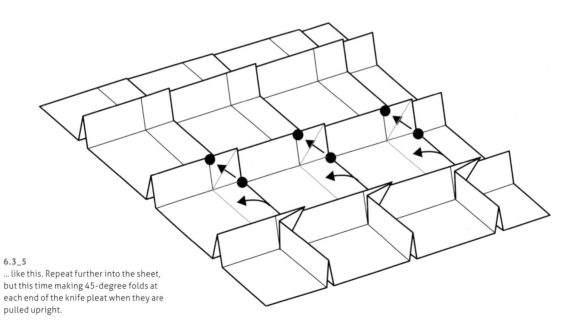

6.3_5
… like this. Repeat further into the sheet,
but this time making 45-degree folds at
each end of the knife pleat when they are
pulled upright.

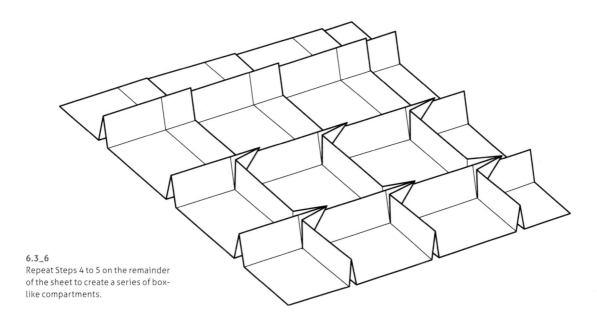

6.3_6
Repeat Steps 4 to 5 on the remainder
of the sheet to create a series of box-
like compartments.

6.4
Cut Pleats
Across Cut Pleats

Lines of cut pleats laid across lines of cut pleats create gridded surface patterns of great intricacy. The feature of bringing the back surface to the front introduces opportunities to use two different colours, images or textures, unique in this book.

6.4_1
For the best effect, use a sheet that has different colours on the two sides.

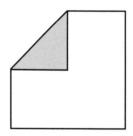

6.4_2
Create six upright pleats, with the mountain folds on the middle and quarter lines.

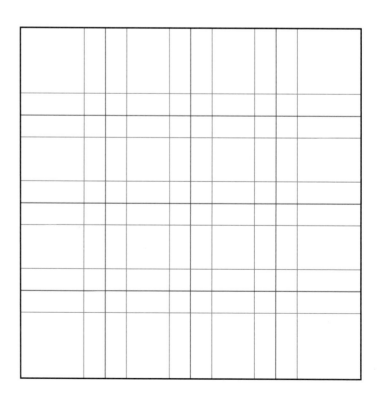

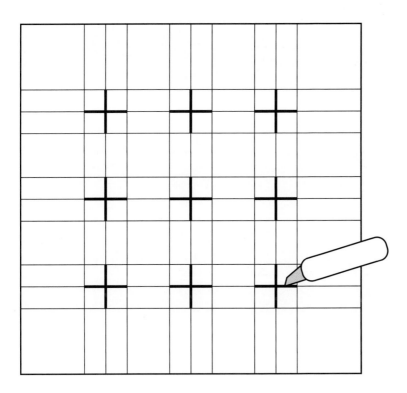

6.4_3
Make a series of short cuts at the
intersections of the upright pleats.

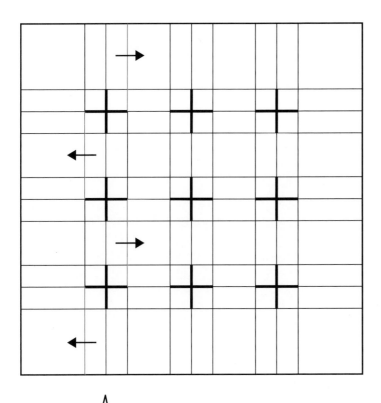

6.4_4
Create a cut pleat in four sections, near the
left-hand edge (see 'Cut Pleats', page 140,
for the method). Flatten the four sections
right-left-right-left, from the top down.

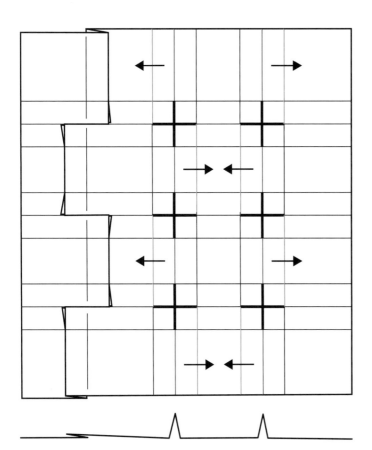

6.4_5
Repeat with the other two vertical pleats. Note that because the top section of the pleat made in the previous step falls to the right, the top section of the neighbouring pleat must fall *the opposite way*, falling to the left. Thus, the second line of pleats is the mirror image of the first line. The third line is the mirror image of the second line ... and so on.

6.4_6
This is the result. Note how the surface appears to be made from a series of rectangles that touch each other.

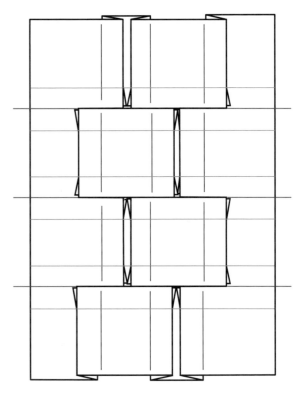

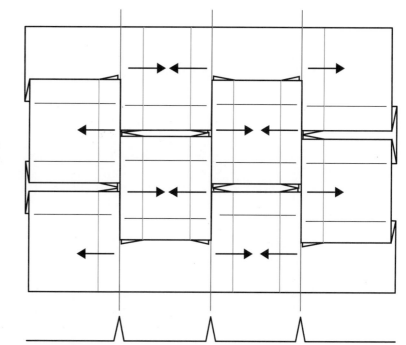

6.4_7
Turn the sheet 90 degrees. Make the other three upright pleats, again flattening each line as a mirror image of its neighbour(s). When upright, a pleat will separate to the left and right, rather like the blooming of a flower.

When this is done, something rather extraordinary happens: the colour from the back of the sheet appears in the middle of each bloom! It's a pretty and wholly unexpected revelation of colour.

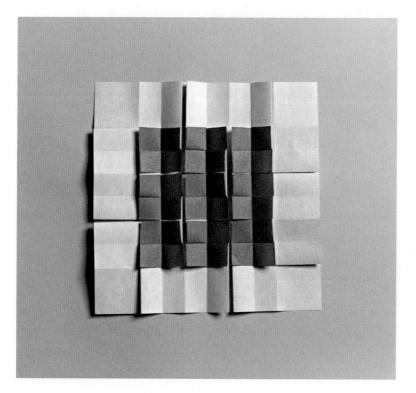

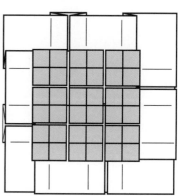

6.4_8
This is the final result. If it will not lie flat, turn the sheet over and rub it, reinforcing the folds.

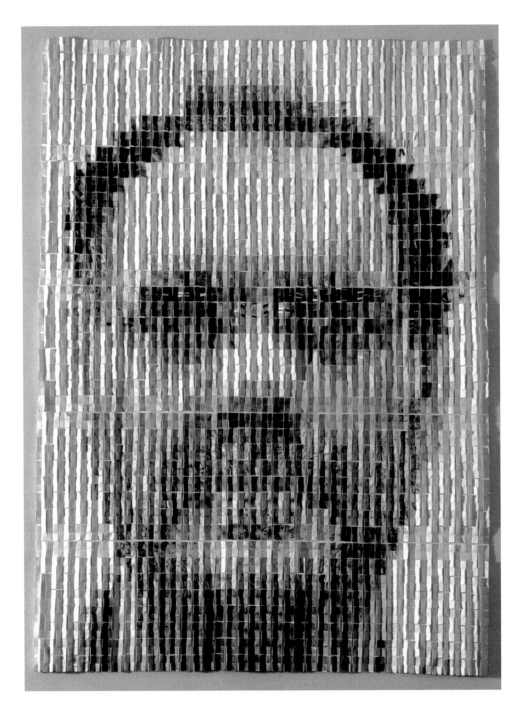

A series of 25 small prints were joined together, each containing a part of the image. The cut-pleats-across-cut-pleats technique described on previous spreads is used to twist parts of the image from the front surface through to be visible on the back. The two sides of the same piece of work resemble the two sides of a flag. From beginning to end, the image halves in height and width. Dimensions: 75 x 50cm (30 x 20in). Designed by Paul Jackson (UK).

7

HOW TO PLEAT FABRIC

7.1

Steaming and Baking

7.1.1　Steam

Steam is the traditional way in which pleats are fixed permanently into fabric. The process is commonly known as plissé. However, the pleats are only 100 per cent permanent if the fabric is 100 per cent synthetic. This is because the high temperature of the steam melts the fibres as they bend across a fold, fixing the fibres – and thus the folds – into position.

When steamed, synthetic fibres will melt, but natural fibres will not. When the fabric is washed, even a high-temperature wash is not hot enough to melt the fibres, so the fabric remains pleated. If natural fibres are used, or if the fabric is a mix of natural and synthetic fibres, the fibres will not melt sufficiently (or even at all) when steamed and will not pleat permanently. So, although such a fabric will appear to have been successfully pleated after steaming, it will relax flat when washed.

It is therefore essential to use a synthetic fabric when steaming. The most commonly used fabric is 100 per cent polyester, although any synthetic fabric is acceptable. Common sense says that if the fabric has a very open weave or is very thick, it will not pleat as successfully as a thin but solid fabric such as might be used to make a shirt or dress.

Therefore, if you intend to wash what you make, never steam natural fibres such as cotton, wool, linen or silk. Always use 100 per cent synthetic fibres.

A few small, family-owned plissé ateliers, run by highly skilled artisans, survive in the fashion capitals of the world. Ateliers can also sometimes be found in other major cities and there are now, unsurprisingly, several plissé factories in East Asia. The experience and skill of a professional plisseur is beyond question. If you need the highest-quality work, or work made in any volume, working with the professionals may be the best option.

These ateliers and factories use large, specialist steam ovens, and the process cannot be easily duplicated at home with regular domestic appliances. Nevertheless, there are ways in which the plissé process can be carried out using low-tech methods and a little ingenuity. The next section explains how it is done.

7.1.2   The Plissé Method

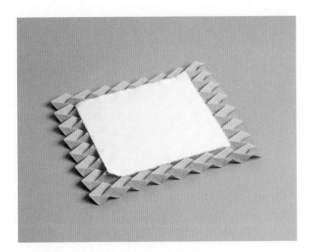

7.1.2_1
From paper, make two masters of the pleat
pattern that is to be made with fabric. The two
masters must be identical. Use paper as heavy
as you can fold, perhaps 200gsm. Place the
fabric on one of the paper sheets. It should be
smaller than the paper (any fabric not trapped
inside the paper will not pleat).

7.1.2_2
Place the other paper sheet on top, meshing
it exactly into the sheet beneath. This traps
the fabric between the layers to create a
three-layer 'sandwich'. It may be helpful to
stretch the paper flat and then pin the fabric
to it in a few places.

7.1.2_3
To ensure that the fabric is trapped cleanly
and evenly, gently massage the sandwich in
your hands, pulling it open and squeezing it
almost shut several times, like this ...

7.1.2_4
... and like this.

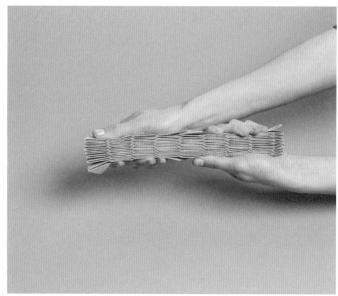

7.1.2_5
When you are satisfied that the three layers
are sitting perfectly together, squeeze the
sandwich very tightly shut.

7.1.2_6
Bind it very tightly with a thread made from
a natural fibre, such as cotton or wool.

7.1.2_7
Bind the sandwich tightly along its full
length. Tie a knot to hold it tight shut and
cut off any excess length of thread.

7.1.2_8
The fabric may now be steamed. Set a domestic steam iron on high. If the fabric has a plastic base, hover the iron 1cm (⅜in) above the pleated surface of the sandwich, ejecting steam. The hovering is to protect the plate from any non-natural substances that may melt on to it. If the plate is metal – as is common on an industrial steam iron – then you may touch the paper with it.

Iron the surface for at least two minutes – longer if the fabric is thick or if the sandwich is large and dense. Turn the sandwich over and steam the other pleated surface. Keep the iron moving slowly and be sure to iron evenly. Do not press hard. Make sure that the steam is being frequently ejected.

7.1.2_9
After steaming, allow the sandwich to cool. Remove the bindings. Carefully separate the two layers of paper to reveal the pleated fabric inside. This is always a magic moment!

7.1.2_10
This is the result. Done well, the fabric will be very crisply pleated, but also remarkably flexible. Pulled open, it will magically snap back into its pleated form.

The example shown here is small, but steaming will also work with very long lengths of fabric sandwiched between large sheets of paper. This is the primary advantage of using the iron method over the baking method (see page 287) – the fabric can be exceptionally long, as required.

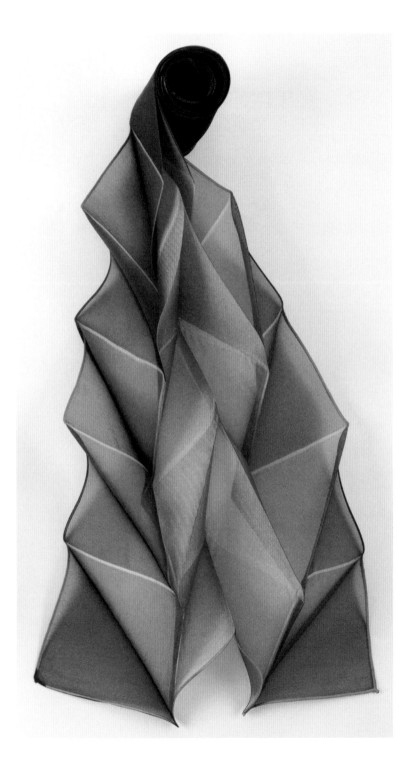

Made using the plissé technique in 100 per cent polyester, this delicate-looking yet sharply folded scarf can be rolled into a cylinder for easy storage. Dimensions when unfolded: 195 x 45cm (78 x 18in). Designed by Reiko Sudo (Japan).

7.1.3   Baking

The traditional plissé technique of using steam to melt synthetic fabrics can also be done with heat, in a regular domestic oven. This alternative method may seem foolhardy, and even dangerous, but done carefully and with a watchful eye, it is as safe as using potentially scalding steam and/or a hot iron. It is easier than steaming, and the only equipment needed is an oven.

The technique is essentially the same as for the steam process, described above, in which the fabric to be pleated is sandwiched between two identically pleated sheets of paper. The three layers are compressed tightly together and bound firmly shut. It is recommended to bind with 100 per cent cotton thread, not a synthetic thread. Follow the description above, exactly, which describes how the three-layer sandwich is made. Be careful to remove any metal pins or clips that may have assisted you during the folding up of the sandwich, as they may scorch the fabric while in the oven.

Place the sandwich into a preheated oven, on a wire rack, away from any gas flame or electrical element. Put a tray of water in the bottom of the oven to create a little steam. Depending on the fabric, the pleat pattern, the solidity of the sandwich, the size of the oven and other factors, bake it for 15 to 20 minutes between 160 and 200°C (320–390°F). Take it out, let it cool and separate the layers.

If the temperature is too high or if it bakes for too long, the fabric will begin to brown and the folds will singe. Before this singeing stage is reached, the pleats will begin to feel brittle. Conversely, if the fabric is not baked for long enough or at too low a temperature, the pleat will not be permanent. With a little experimentation and by learning from your successes and failures, you will quickly learn how to control the variables to create a successful pleat. However, the technique is very forgiving and it is not necessary to precisely control the variables to achieve a good result.

The limitation of the technique is that the sandwich needs to be laid out straight on the wire rack, which means that the size of the fabric is limited by the size of the oven. If the fabric is curled up to fit in the oven, it may have a permanent curl when removed. When using a steam iron, the sandwich can be as long as needed.

It is strongly recommended that you keep a vigil in front of the oven during the first baking, to check that nothing is burning up or melting. Once you are satisfied that your folded paper templates, the fabric between them and the binding thread remain stable when hot, you can be more relaxed about the process and not keep a constant watch. Keep a pair of oven gloves to hand and be careful when removing the sandwich from the oven at the end – that you don't knock it off its rack into the water beneath, something very easily done when wearing oven gloves!

7.2

Shadowfolds

'Shadowfolds' is an extraordinary technique devised by the origami artist and designer, Chris K. Palmer, which combines the techniques of traditional fabric smocking with the 'Twist Folding' techniques developed and popularized by the Japanese origami master Shuzo Fujimoto in the 1970s. Twist folding in paper is laborious and exacting, but when the twists are made in fabric with a needle and thread using the Shadowfolds method, it becomes a delightfully quick, simple and magical technique. Each arm of each twist is a simple knife pleat, which is why the technique merits a place in this book.

This section will explain the basic Shadowfold method with a single square twist, followed by single triangular and hexagonal variations, and concluding with techniques for creating multiple twists. More information can be found in the book *Shadowfolds*, written by Jeffrey Rutzky and Chris K. Palmer. For practice, use a plain, light-coloured fabric, not too soft, either natural or artificial, about 30 x 30cm (12 x 12in).

7.2.1 The Square Twist

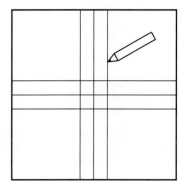

7.2.1_1
On a sheet of paper, draw six lines as shown. The drawing may also be made with CAD and printed after Step 3.

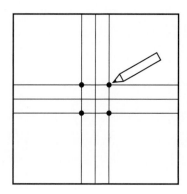

7.2.1_2
Mark the corners of the central square with dots.

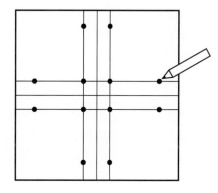

7.2.1_3
Create four pairs of dots as shown here, perpendicular to the lines. Their exact opposition is unimportant, but they must be further away from the central square than the size of the square itself.

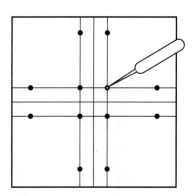

7.2.1_4
Using a tool such as an awl or a sharp pencil, prick small holes in the centre of each of the 12 dots.

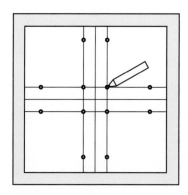

7.2.1_5
The blue square represents the fabric, which should be approximately the size of the drawing. Place the drawing on the fabric and secure it with pins or tape. With a pencil, or perhaps chalk, make a small dot on the fabric through each pricked hole.

7.2.1_6
This is the fabric, complete with dots. An alternative method is to make the drawing on paper and, instead of pricking the holes, to place the drawing under the fabric on a lightbox and to draw the dots directly on to the fabric using the strong light from underneath as a guide. A window makes an excellent alternative for a lightbox.

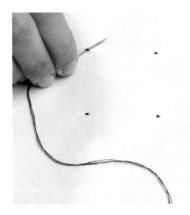

7.2.1_7
Using a needle and thread, pick up just one or two fabric threads at one of the dots in the centre. The cotton is black so it can be seen in the photographs, but it is probably better to use cotton in a colour that matches the fabric.

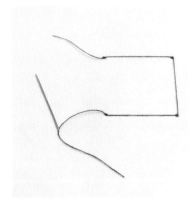

7.2.1_8
Similarly, pick up one or two threads at the other dots in the square.

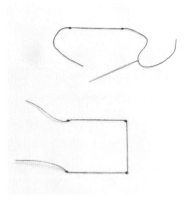

7.2.1_9
Pick up one or two threads at a pair of dots.

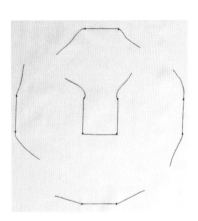

7.2.1_10
Repeat with the other pairs of dots. The stitching is now complete.

7.2.1_11
Gather up the ends of the thread in the central square and begin to tie them together with a simple overhand knot. Pull the knot very tight and secure it with a second knot. All four corners of the square must be pulled tightly together. The fabric will look untidy, but this is normal.

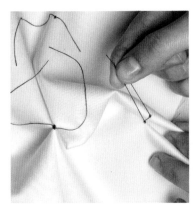

7.2.1_12
Similarly, pull together two threaded dots near the edge. Pull them tightly together and secure them with two overhand knots.

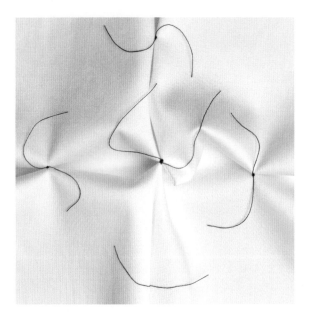

7.2.1_13
Repeat with the other three pairs. This is the result. The fabric will probably look very untidy, but this is normal. Turn over.

7.2.1_14
This is the front side. If any fabric is trapped inside the central square, pull it out to the front side so that all of the surface of the fabric can be seen.

7.2.1_15
Slowly stretch flat the fabric in the centre. The untidy heap of folds will gradually transform itself into a neat and tidy flat square ...

7.2.1_16
... like this. It is critical to understand that the four pleats that radiate away from the central twisted square must fall flat either all clockwise or all anti-clockwise, not a mix of the two directions. In the photograph, the pleats fall anti-clockwise.

7.2.1_17
This is the completed twist, ironed flat. When ironed, the twist is pleasingly geometric. If the pleats are long, add more pairs of dots at regular intervals along their length, to help keep them in an accurate shape. All the stitches may now be removed. The astute reader may notice that a Shadowfolds twist is a copy of the Cut Pleat (see page 140), but without the cuts.

7.2.2   Other Twists

The square twist above can be adapted so that
other polygons will twist flat. Here are two common
examples – an equilateral triangle and a hexagon.
The methods for making them are exactly the same
as for the twisted squares.

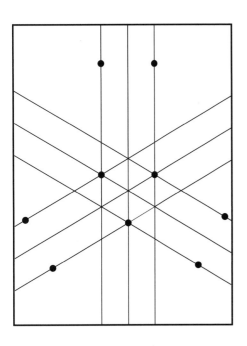

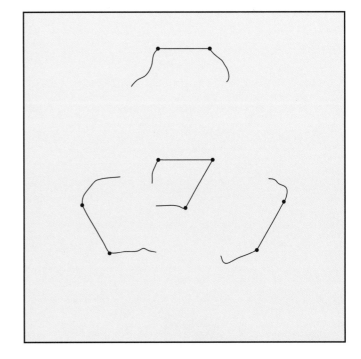

7.2.2_1
Draw three sets of three parallel lines,
rotating 120 degrees between each set of
lines. Add dots where shown: three in the
centre and three pairs. Transfer the dot
pattern to the fabric and pick up the fabric,
making stitches where shown. Pull tight the
triangle in the centre, bringing the dots
together. Tie them with two tight overhand
knots. Also tie together and knot the three
pairs of dots that are around the edge. Turn
over and arrange the triangular twist to look
like the photograph.

7.2.2_2
This is the completed triangular twist.
Note that this time, the three pleats are
rotating in a clockwise direction, whereas
the four pleats in the square twist rotate
anti-clockwise.

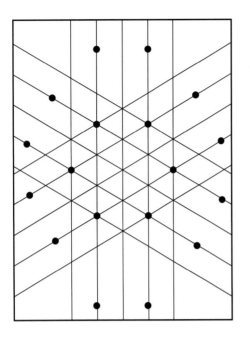

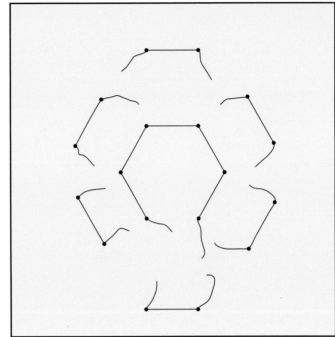

7.2.2_3
Draw three sets of five parallel lines, rotating
120 degrees between each set of lines. Add
dots where shown: six in the centre and six
pairs near the edge. Transfer the dot pattern
to the fabric and pick up the fabric, making
stitches where shown. Pull tight the hexagon
in the centre, bringing the dots together. Tie
them with two tight overhand knots. Also
tie together and knot the six pairs of dots
around the edge. Turn over and arrange the
hexagonal twist to look like the photograph,
making sure that the hexagon has twisted as
far and as flat as it will rotate.

7.2.2_4
The hexagonal twist complete and ironed
flat. Note that the six pleats are rotating
anti-clockwise.

7.2.3   Twists in Combination

The Shadowfolds technique comes alive when twists are used in combination. There are strict rules that govern how one twist can connect with another based on the principles of tessellating a two-dimensional surface, but these limitations are surprisingly broad, and many fascinating patterns can be developed.

Here are two of the simplest patterns, showing how squares can connect in a 90-degree grid and how triangles can connect in a 60/120-degree grid.

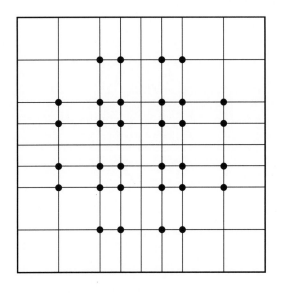

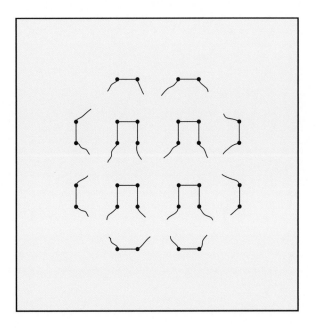

7.2.3_1
Draw a set of five equally spaced vertical lines across the middle and a sixth and seventh further out to the left and right. Repeat, creating seven horizontal lines. Draw four squares of dots as shown and eight further pairs, near the edges. With fabric, thread the four squares and the eight pairs in the way described previously. Knot them as before. Turn over, twist the four squares flat and arrange the eight pleats. Look at the photograph on the next page to check what you are trying to achieve.

7.2.3_2
This is the square grid. Note how the top left-hand and bottom right-hand pleats twist anti-clockwise and the others twist clockwise. The strict rule is that neighbouring twists must rotate flat in opposite directions. This applies to any polygon, not just to squares. The grid could repeat infinitely. The twists can be closer together or further apart, as you wish. Instead of a grid, the twists could also be in a single line, like a line of buttons.

It is essential that the grid is drawn accurately. If your grid is large and complex, make it as a CAD drawing and print it on over-size paper, using a plotter.

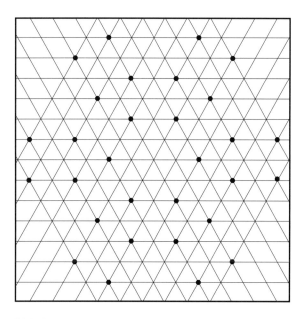

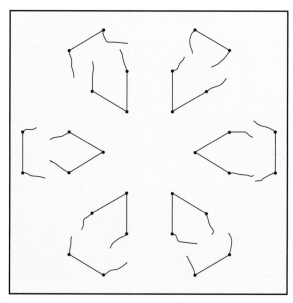

7.2.3_3
Draw a grid of equilateral triangles, as shown. There must be a set of at least 13 parallel lines in each of the three directions. Make dots that define six equilateral triangles around the centre point, and a further six pairs of dots near the edges. Be careful to follow the drawing exactly.

With fabric, thread the six triangles and the six pairs, pull each tight and tie them off, as described previously. Turn over and twist the triangles flat. Check the photograph to see what you are trying to achieve.

7.2.3_4

This is the triangular grid, not in the shape of a triangle, as might be expected, but in the shape of a hexagon. Note that if one triangle twists flat in a clockwise direction, its neighbours to either side will both twist flat in an anti-clockwise direction (or vice versa). This is the same rule as seen in the square grid above, but applied to a triangular grid.

This grid could extend infinitely as a series of connected hexagons (much like a beehive), with a twisted triangle at each corner of each hexagon. The triangles could also be closer together or further apart, so long as the grid is a consistent size throughout.

Here, the twists-in-combination technique places many
twisted shadowfold squares together. When the twists
are placed in careful relation to the vertical stripes, they
create a new pattern of coloured squares, each of which is
made from sections of four twisted squares. Designed by
Shahar Avnet. Student project, Department of Fashion
Design, Shenkar College, Tel Aviv (Israel).

A fascinating arrangement of triangles, squares and
hexagons create a complex example of shadowfold twists.
Back lighting reveals the beauty of the pattern. There are
many ways to twist different polygons in combination.
Designed by Jeff Rutsky (USA).

7.3

Other Techniques

7.3.1   Stitching

One way to hold a fold in place in any fabric is to run
a stitch along its length to prevent it unfolding.

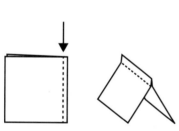

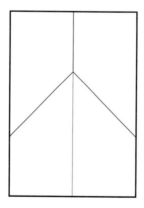

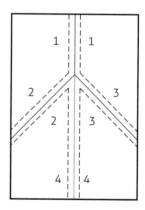

7.3.1_1
The technique is particularly effective for
pleats in which no fold touches any other
fold, such as an accordion, knife or box pleat.
Each fold in the pleat can be stitched
separately and independently of all the
others. It is your choice whether the fabric
is stitched very close to the folded edge or
some distance away. These separately made
folds can be stitched quickly with a sewing
machine. Hand stitching is an option, but the
process can be unnecessarily laborious.

7.3.1_2
The technique becomes a little more complex
when making V-pleats, or any pleated pattern
in which mountain and valley folds touch or
cross each other. The stitched lines
converging on each other from different
directions can potentially create a misshapen
node and care must be taken to devise a
stitching pattern that does not distort the
surface of the fabric, the folded edges or the
node. For this reason, the stitching is often
better done by hand than with a sewing
machine, so that the stitching around the
node can be controlled precisely.

To stitch a basic V-pleat, first stitch 1 against
1, 2 against 2, and 3 against 3. These are the
three mountain folds that converge at the
node. The fourth fold, by contrast, is a valley
and must be stitched by turning the fabric
over so that the fold is a mountain. Thus,
when stitching 4 against 4, be sure to do so
on the reverse side.

7.3.2   Interfacing

Interfacing is a stiff material that can be stitched or fused by heat to the back of a chosen fabric, to stiffen and/or strengthen it. It is commonly used inside collars, or where fabric needs to be strengthened, or where the surface will likely shrink or stretch out of shape. For general use, non-woven interfacing is preferable to woven. Interfacing comes in several different weights, so choose one that is the same weight as your fabric, or a little lighter, but not heavier.

Interfacing can be introduced to the back of a pleated surface to considerably improve its ability to create and retain a folded edge. However, by itself, it will not make a pleat permanent, so you may still need to stitch it (see opposite). Steaming the interfacing to achieve a permanent pleat can be problematic as it can melt like grilled cheese, dirtying your iron. Experiment with small pieces to see if your combination of interfacing, steam iron and fabric will be successful.

7.3.3   Starch

The starching of clothes, napkins and quilts was common in former times, but is rarely done today. It must be remembered that while starch will stiffen a fabric, it will rinse out when the fabric is washed and the stiffness will disappear. So, using starch is recommended only if you do not intend to wash what you have made.

However, starch has one useful attribute for pleating: when a fabric is sprayed with starch, it is then unlikely to warp out of shape. Thus, if you wish to make precisely aligned pleats, first starch the fabric and then cut it to shape. This will keep all the edges straight and measuring will be much easier. The starch can be washed out later.

7.3.4   Unorthodox Methods

The methods described here are tried and tested; used appropriately, they will create permanent pleats in fabric. However, there are many other feasible methods for creating pleats, some of which use fabric and some of which do not. Here are some of those methods:

Hold a pleat in place or hold it flat with buttons, Velcro, poppers, toggles, magnets or other fastenings. How many different methods of fastening are there?

Make each polygon within a pleat pattern from a separate piece and join them together. The polygons can be made from a stiff material, sandwiched between flexible fabric. The flexibility of the fabric will enable pleats to form.

Make a wire frame of the pleated form. Any nodes (such as on a V-pleat) can be made to articulate, or can be fixed into position, permanently.

There are, of course, no limits to the ways in which pleats can be formed and held in place. Set your imagination free and see what you can devise. Assume no limits.

Even if your pleating pattern is simple and familiar, if it is made with an unusual material, and/or if the pleats are held in place by unusual means, you will have created an original piece of work. So, if you consider your folding abilities to be limited, focus instead on making simple pleat patterns in an interesting way. Experience has shown time and again that much of the best pleated work is not necessarily made by folding virtuosos, but by those with a sensitivity for materials and good making skills.

Photo Credits
All photography of pleat techniques and
step-by-step hand sequences throughout
the book by Meidad Sochovolski.

p.7 ©Angharad McLaren
p.15 ©Andrea Russo
pp.52–53 Erik & Marty Demaine
p.57 Elisheva Fineman
p.58t Scenic Architecture. Photography: Shen Zhonghai
pp.58–59 Kengo Kuma & Associates.
p.59 ZIG ZAG chair by G. T. Rietveld, Cassina 1093
(drawing 1934) © DACS 2014.
p.72 Design & Fabrication by Randy Weersing.
Photography: Randy Weersing
p.74 Benjamin Hubert Ltd.
p.82 Courtesy BHLDN. Model: Sheila Marquez
at Supreme Management
p.83 Artwork by Richard Sweeney. Photography:
Richard Sweeney
pp.84–85 Architect: J. J. Pan & Partners, Architects &
Planners. Photography: Jeffrey Cheng Photograph
pp.90–91 ©Chris Hardy
p.95 Rebecca Guiseking
p.99 ©Molo
pp.100–01 ©Molo
pp.108–09 Kevin Box
pp.112–13 Iris Haggai
p.114 (both images) Meidad Sochovolski
p.120t Anne Kyyrö Quinn, Leaf Design.
Photography: Marek Sikora
p.120b Anne Kyyrö Quinn, Leaf Design.
Photography: Riitta Sourander
p.121 Photographer: Chris Moore. Designer: Alice Palmer
p.126 Architect: Hironaka Ogawa/Hironaka Ogawa &
Associates. Photography: Daici Ano
p.127 Architect: Hironaka Ogawa/Hironaka Ogawa &
Associates. Photography: Daici Ano
p.130 © VIEW Pictures Ltd / Alamy
p.131 Adrian Holme
p.134 Matthew Shlian
p.139 Erik & Marty Demaine
pp.150–51 Meidad Sochovolski
p.151 Meidad Sochovolski
pp.153–54 IN-EI by Issey Miyake for Artemide.
Photography: Miro Zagnoli
p.158 IN-EI by Issey Miyake for Artemide.
Photography: Miro Zagnoli
p.159 Philip Chapman-Bell
p.174 Project LAMPSHADO. Photography: Simona
Tomaskova Gleissnerova
pp.178–79 ©Milo Keller / www.milokeller.com

p.189 ©Tine De Ruysser
pp.192–93 Arktura Pleat Coffee Table, designed by
Chris Kabatsi
p.196 ©Eiko Ozawa/Dancing Grey Studio
p.197 Meidad Sochovolski
p.199 Patrik Tamm
pp.206–07 Design: Four O Nine. Manufacturing
and distribution: Nienkamper Inc. Photography:
Chris Chapman
p.212 Bloomingville
p.215 (both images) ©Milo Keller /
www.milokeller.com
p.227 Jule Waibel
pp.228–29 Faceture vases by Phil Cuttance.
Images: Petr Krecji
pp.234–35 Adam Berry
p.242 Janine Farber
p.243 K.W.Y. (Ben Allen & Ricardo Gomes)
p.248 From the series 'Punschlos glücklich' by Aldo
Tolino, folded C-print 2013
p.249 Faceture vases by Phil Cuttance. Images:
Petr Krecji
pp.250–51 Goran Konjevod
p.255t Alexandra Wilhelm
p.255b Meidad Sochovolski
p.257 Goran Konjevod
p.258 Goran Konjevod
p 268 Meidad Sochovolski
p.269 Etienne Cliquet
pp.278–79 (both images) Paul Jackson
pp.280–81 Jeff Rutsky
p.286 Reiko Sudo/ NUNO Corporation.
Photography: Keiko Matsubara
p.298 Meidad Sochovolski
p.299 Jeff Rutsky
p.304 ©Cathy Hartt

Acknowledgements

Across the years, I have run many workshops and courses for students of design on the theme of pleating, first from 1982 to 2001 in many colleges across the UK, and since 2001, primarily at Shenkar College of Engineering and Design in Tel Aviv. The sum of what I have learnt from my students has formed the structure and content of this book, and for that guidance I am profoundly grateful.

From Shenkar, I must thank Leah Perez, Head of the Fashion Department, and Uri Tsaig and Dr Katya Oicherman, the past and present Heads of the Textile Department, for their generous and continued support of my teaching, and their students, who tolerated my occasionally eccentric teaching experiments in pursuit of The Perfect Course and who, despite or because of me, made so much beautiful work. In many ways, I feel this is our book, not my book alone. I must give special thanks to my students Nitsan Greyevski and Dror Zac, who prepared samples for the Shadowfolds and fabric steaming sections of the book, respectively.

I must also thank Meidad Sochovolski for his beautiful photography, my editor Peter Jones for his light but accurate guidance, &Smith for their superb layout of my complex manuscript and most of all, Jo Lightfoot at LKP for having the faith to commission the book.

Finally, I must thank my wife Miri Golan for her support during the two years I was writing the book, and our son Jonathan for patiently allowing me extra time in the studio when we should have been building gliders together.